THE WHITE DARKNESS

ALSO BY DAVID GRANN

The Lost City of Z

The Devil and Sherlock Holmes

Killers of the Flower Moon

The Old Man and the Gun

DAVID GRANN

THE WHITE DARKNESS

**SIMON &
SCHUSTER**

London · New York · Sydney · Toronto · New Delhi

A CBS COMPANY

First published in the United States by Doubleday, a division of
Penguin Random House LLC, 2018
First published in Great Britain by Simon & Schuster UK Ltd, 2018
A CBS COMPANY

This work originally appeared in *The New Yorker* on 12 and 19 February 2018.

1 3 5 7 9 10 8 6 4 2

Simon & Schuster UK Ltd
1st Floor
222 Gray's Inn Road
London WC1X 8HB

www.simonandschuster.co.uk
www.simonandschuster.com.au
www.simonandschuster.co.in

Simon & Schuster Australia, Sydney
Simon & Schuster India, New Delhi

A CIP catalogue record for this book
is available from the British Library

Hardback ISBN: 978-1-4711-7802-3
eBook ISBN: 978-1-4711-7803-0

Book design by Pei Loi Koay
Printed and bound by CPI Group (UK) Ltd, Croydon, CR0 4YY

MIX
Paper from
responsible sources
FSC® C020471

Simon & Schuster UK Ltd are committed to sourcing paper that is made
from wood grown in sustainable forests and support the Forest Stewardship Council,
the leading international forest certification organisation. Our books
displaying the FSC logo are printed on FSC certified paper.

For Joanna, Max, and Alicia

"There is nothing to see but white darkness."

—HENRY WORSLEY

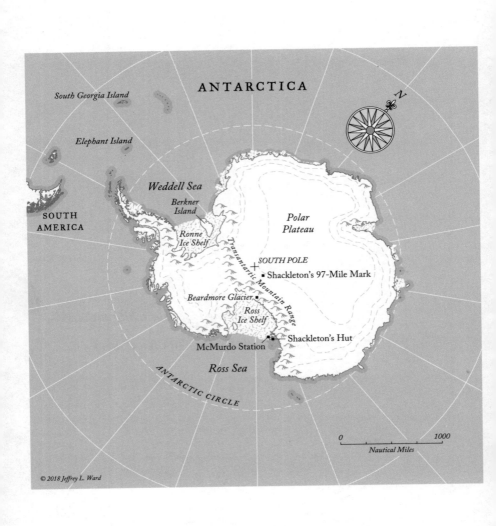

ANTARCTICA

South Georgia Island

Elephant Island

Weddell Sea

Berkner
Island

SOUTH
AMERICA

Ronne
Ice Shelf

Polar
Plateau

Transantarctic Mountain Range

SOUTH POLE

■ Shackleton's 97-Mile Mark

Beardmore Glacier ■

Ross
Ice Shelf

■ Shackleton's Hut

McMurdo Station ■

Ross Sea

ANTARCTIC CIRCLE

0   1000

Nautical Miles

© 2018 Jeffrey L. Ward

CONTENTS

I | MORTAL DANGER

THE MAN FELT LIKE A SPECK IN THE FROZEN NOTHINGNESS. Every direction he turned, he could see ice stretching to the edge of the Earth: white ice and blue ice, glacial-ice tongues and ice wedges. There were no living creatures in sight. Not a seal or even a bird. Nothing but him.

It was hard to breathe, and each time he exhaled the moisture froze on his face: a chandelier of crystals hung from his beard; his eyebrows were encased like preserved specimens; his eyelashes cracked when he blinked. Get wet and you die, he often reminded himself. The temperature was nearly minus forty degrees

Fahrenheit, and it felt far colder because of the wind, which sometimes whipped icy particles into a blinding cloud, making him so disoriented that he toppled over, his bones rattling against the ground.

The man, whose name was Henry Worsley, consulted a GPS device to determine precisely where he was. According to his coordinates, he was on the Titan Dome, an ice formation near the South Pole that rises more than ten thousand feet above sea level. Sixty-two days earlier, on November 13, 2015, he'd set out from the coast of Antarctica, hoping to achieve what his hero, Ernest Shackleton, had failed to do a century earlier: to trek on foot from one side of the continent to the other. The journey, which would pass through the South Pole, was more than a thousand miles, and would traverse what is arguably the most brutal environment in the world. And, whereas Shackleton had been part of a large expedition, Worsley, who was fifty-five, was crossing alone and unsupported: no food caches had been deposited along the route to help him forestall starvation, and he had to haul all his provisions on a sled, without the assistance of dogs or a sail. Nobody had attempted this feat before.

Worsley's sled—which, at the outset, weighed three hundred and twenty-five pounds, nearly double his own weight—was attached to a harness around his waist, and to drag it across the ice he wore cross-country skis and pushed forward with poles in each hand. The trek had begun at nearly sea level, and he'd been ascending with a merciless steadiness, the air thinning and his nose sometimes bleeding from the pressure; a crimson mist colored the snow along his path. When the terrain became too steep, he removed his skis and trudged on foot, his boots fitted with crampons to grip the ice. His eyes scanned the surface for crevasses. One misstep and he'd vanish into a hidden chasm.

Worsley was a retired British Army officer who had served in the Special Air Service, a renowned commando unit. He was also a sculptor, a fierce boxer, a photographer who meticulously documented his travels, a horticulturalist, a collector of rare books and maps and fossils, and an amateur historian who had become a leading authority on Shackleton. On the ice, though, he resembled a beast, hauling and sleeping, hauling and sleeping, as if he were keeping time to some primal rhythm.

He had grown accustomed to the obliterating conditions, overcoming miseries that would've broken just about anyone else. He mentally painted images onto the desolate landscape for hours on end, and he summoned memories of his wife, Joanna, his twenty-one-year-old son, Max, and his nineteen-year-old daughter, Alicia. They had scrawled inspiring messages on his skis. One contained the adage "Success is not final, failure is not fatal: it is the courage to continue that counts." Another, written by Joanna, said, "Come back to me safely, my darling."

As is true of many adventurers, he seemed to be on an inward quest as much as an outward one—the journey was a way to

Henry Worsley in Antarctica.

subject himself to an ultimate test of character. He was also raising
money for the Endeavour Fund, a charity for wounded soldiers.
A few weeks earlier, Prince William, the Duke of Cambridge,
who was the patron of the expedition, had broadcast a message
for Worsley that said, "You're doing a cracking job. Everyone
back here is keeping up with what you're up to, and very proud of
everything you're achieving."

Worsley's journey captivated people around the world, including
legions of schoolchildren who were following his progress. Each
day, after trekking for several hours and burrowing into his tent,
he relayed a short audio broadcast about his experiences. (He
performed this bit of modern magic by calling, on his satellite
phone, a friend in England, who recorded the dispatch and then
posted it on Worsley's website.) His voice, cool and unwavering,
enthralled listeners. One evening, two weeks into his journey,
he said:

I overslept a little this morning, which, actually, I was grateful
for, as the previous forty-eight hours' labor has been hugely
draining. But what greeted me opening the tent flap was not
my favorite scene: total whiteout and driving snow borne on
an easterly wind. And so it remained all day and has showed
no sliver of change this evening. Navigation under such
circumstances is always a challenge. I certainly made a dog's
breakfast of the first three hours, at one stage wondering why

the wind had suddenly switched from the east to the north. Stupid error! The wind hadn't changed direction—*I* had. I reckon I lost about three miles' distance today from snaking around, head permanently bowed to read the compass, just my shuffling skis to look at for nine hours. Anyway, I'm back on track and now happy I can part a straight line, even through another day of the white darkness.

By the middle of January 2016, he had travelled more than eight hundred miles, and virtually every part of him was in agony. His arms and legs throbbed. His back ached. His feet were blistered and his toenails were discolored. His fingers had started to become numb with frostbite. In his diary, he wrote, "Am worried about my fingers—one tip of little finger already gone and all others very sore." One of his front teeth had broken off, and the wind whistled through the gap. He had lost some forty pounds, and he became fixated on his favorite foods, listing them for his broadcast listeners: "Fish pie, brown bread, double cream, steaks and chips, more chips, smoked salmon, baked potato, eggs, rice pudding, Dairy Milk chocolate, tomatoes, bananas, apples, anchovies, Shredded Wheat, Weetabix, brown sugar, peanut butter, honey, toast, pasta, pizza and pizza. Ahhhhh!"

He was on the verge of collapse. Yet he was never one to give up, and adhered to the SAS's unofficial motto, "Always a little further"—a line from James Elroy Flecker's 1913 poem "The

Golden Journey to Samarkand." The motto was painted on the front of Worsley's sled, and he murmured it to himself like a mantra: "Always a little further . . . a little further."

He had just reached the summit of the Titan Dome and was beginning to descend, the force of gravity propelling him toward his destination, which was only about a hundred miles away. He was so close to what he liked to call a "rendezvous with history." Yet how much farther could he press on before the cold consumed him? He had studied with devotion the decision-making of Shackleton, whose ability to escape mortal danger was legendary, and who had famously saved the life of his entire crew when an expedition went awry. Whenever Worsley faced a perilous situation—and he was now in more peril than he'd ever been—he asked himself one question: What would Shacks do?

II | THE LURE OF LITTLE VOICES

HENRY WORSLEY'S FATHER, LIKE SHACKLETON, HAD been a celebrated leader of men. While growing up, Henry had heard stories about how his father, Richard Worsley, had fought with distinction during the Second World War, helping his regiment win battles in the deserts of North Africa and on the streets of Italy. *The Independent* had praised his ability to maintain "morale in bruising situations." Over the years, he had risen to the highest ranks of the British Army, becoming Quartermaster-General in 1979.

"We had seen God in his splendors," Shackleton
wrote of his trans-Antarctic expedition.

To Henry, his father often seemed like a biblical force: commanding, revered, looming but absent. A relative recalled, "Henry barely saw his dad, and when he did it was, like, shaking his hand. It wasn't like a hug or like love or anything like that." Richard Worsley was often posted overseas, and when Henry was seven he was sent to a boarding school for boys, in Kent.

Henry, who was slight, with unnervingly steady blue eyes, found solace in sports, excelling at cricket, rugby, skiing, and hockey. Although he was not physically overpowering, he competed as if something were gnawing at him, diving head first after balls and skiing off marked trails to plunge through murderous woods.

At the age of thirteen, he moved to the Stowe School, in Buckinghamshire, where he was the captain of the cricket, rugby, and hockey teams. Kids tended to follow him around, but he preferred to wander alone across the school grounds—forests and meadows that spanned seven hundred and fifty acres. He hunted for birds' nests, marking their locations on a map. Every few days, he checked on them, jotting down in a notebook how many eggs had been laid, or how fast the hatchlings were growing.

He had little interest in his classroom studies, but he often disappeared into the library and read poetry and tales of adventure. One day, he retrieved a copy of *The Heart of the Antarctic*, Shackleton's account of his gallant but doomed attempt, in 1907–1909, to reach the South Pole. (The journey was known as the *Nimrod* expedition, for the ship he had commanded.) Worsley read the opening lines: "Men go out into the void spaces of the world for various reasons. Some are actuated simply by a love of adventure, some have the keen thirst for scientific knowledge, and others again are drawn away from the trodden paths by the 'lure of little voices,' the mysterious fascination of the unknown." The book was illustrated with photographs from the expedition, and Worsley stared at them in wonder. There was the hut, crammed with a stove and canned goods and a phonograph, where Shackleton and his men had wintered on Ross Island, off the coast of Antarctica. There were the Manchurian ponies that had been brought to pull sleds but soon succumbed. And there, walking across the majestic deathscape, was Shackleton, a broad-shouldered, handsome man who seemed to embody the motto on his family crest, *Fortitudine Vincimus:* "By Endurance We Conquer."

Worsley read everything he could about Shackleton and other polar explorers. He was delighted to discover that Frank Worsley, a trusted member of one of Shackleton's expeditions, was a distant relative of his, and had written his own thrilling memoir, in which he described braving an "unending series of blizzards, gales and blinding snowstorms."

In 1978, Henry Worsley graduated from Stowe. Though he burned to become a polar explorer, he enlisted in the Army. His mother, Sally, recalled, "He definitely didn't want to go into the Army, but then we sort of persuaded him that he might enjoy it and why not give it a go." He attended the Royal Military

Henry Worsley, like his father,
joined the Army.

Academy Sandhurst, in Surrey, where
he trained to become an officer. At
his graduation ceremony, in 1980, he
was paraded past some of the Army's
military brass, including his father,
who, in 1976, had been knighted.
Henry snapped his hand to his
forehead in salute.

Henry became a second lieutenant,
and was assigned to the same regiment
in which his father had once served.
During this period, he began to revisit
the stories of Shackleton, which he
no longer considered merely romantic
tales. "I became mesmerized by the
extraordinary levels of hardship
these men were prepared to endure,"
Worsley later wrote in a book, *In
Shackleton's Footsteps,* which was published in 2011. "Shackleton had
become more than a hero to me," he noted. "I looked upon him
as a mentor. I was going into the business of leading men and as
a nineteen-year-old, new to his trade, I believed that there was no
better example to follow than his."

III | HELL IS A COLD PLACE

ERNEST SHACKLETON WAS, IN MANY WAYS, A FAILURE. His initial foray into polar exploration came in 1901, when he joined an expedition led by Robert Falcon Scott, who hoped to become the first person to reach the South Pole—a place that, in Scott's words, had "hitherto been untrodden by human feet, unseen by human eyes." Scott, a British naval officer, was a dogged and courageous commander, and committed to scientific inquiry. Yet he could also be dogmatic, distant, and bullying, ruling over the members of his party with the kind of absolute authority to which he had grown accustomed in the Navy. He once ordered that a cook be put in irons for insubordination, noting that the punishment instilled in the man a "condition of whining humility." Shackleton, who had served a decade in the merchant marine, bridled against such overbearing methods.

In February 1902, the group set up a base camp on the frozen rim of Antarctica. The continent has two seasons: summer, which lasts from November to February, and winter. For much of the summer, because of the tilt of the Earth, sunlight lingers through the night. In winter, the darkness is enveloping and the conditions are even more anathema to human life; the temperature one July was recorded at minus a hundred and twenty-eight degrees. And so Scott waited until November 2, when the summer light began to grace the sky, before he embarked, with Shackleton and a third man, Edward Wilson, on the eight-hundred-mile journey to the Pole—what another member of the expedition called "the

long trail, the lone trail, the outward trail, the darkward trail."

As the three men walked, they were blinded by the polar glare, and their flesh was eaten away by hunger, frostbite, and scurvy. Scott frequently lashed out at his men, once shouting, "Come here, you bloody fools!" Shackleton responded, "You're the worst bloody fool of the lot."

On December 31, 1902, more than four hundred and eighty miles from the Pole, Scott gave the order to retreat. As they struggled back, Shackleton was coughing up blood, and by the time he reached their ship he was, as he admitted, "broken."

Four years later, Shackleton, assuming his first command, mounted the *Nimrod* expedition. This time, he and three companions went closer to the South Pole than anyone had previously gone: ninety-seven nautical miles away. (A nautical mile, which is used in polar navigation, is fifteen percent longer than a regular mile.) Yet Shackleton, fearing for his men's welfare, retreated again. After returning to England, he didn't discuss his failure with his wife, Emily, though he said, "A live donkey is better than a dead lion, isn't it?"

"Yes, darling, as far as I am concerned," she replied.

Meanwhile, others made history. In 1909, an American explorer, Robert E. Peary, claimed to have been the first to reach the North Pole. (Whether he made it precisely to the Pole was subsequently disputed.) Two years later, the Norwegian explorer Roald Amundsen won the race to the South Pole. Using teams of dogs instead of men to pull sleds, and often skiing, he beat a party led by Scott by thirty-three days. After Scott discovered a Norwegian flag planted at the Pole, he wrote in his diary, "Great God! This is an awful place."

Scott and his party reached the South Pole on January 18, 1912,
only to discover Amundsen's tent and Norwegian flag.

On the return journey, he
and his four men, including
Edward Wilson, ran out
of food. "We shall die like
gentlemen," Scott scribbled
in his diary, before they all
perished.

With the poles conquered,
Shackleton, who was
approaching forty, turned his
restless attention to what he
considered the sole remaining
prize—a trans-Antarctica
crossing. "From the sentimental
point of view, it is the last great Polar journey that can be made,"
he wrote in a proposal, emphasizing that it would be the "most
striking of all journeys."

Polar expeditions, marked by deprivation and claustrophobia,
serve as a laboratory for testing human dynamics. History
is studded with accounts of members of parties bickering,
backstabbing, slandering, and even, in some cases, mutinying and
murdering. Shackleton, who had witnessed on the Scott expedition
the corrosive tensions among team members, sought recruits with
the qualities that he deemed essential for polar exploration: "First,
optimism; second, patience; third, physical endurance; fourth,

idealism; fifth and last, courage." One person who, Shackleton believed, perfectly reflected these criteria was Frank Worsley. A forty-two-year-old seaman from New Zealand, with a broad chest and a square jaw, he was among the twenty-eight members chosen for the expedition, and Shackleton appointed him captain of the party's ship. "I was committed to my fate," Worsley wrote.

On October 26, 1914, the ship—a hundred-and-forty-foot wooden schooner rechristened the *Endurance,* after Shackleton's family motto—set out from Argentina, carrying the men and three lifeboats. Ten days later, the expedition stopped at South Georgia, a glacier-covered island about eleven hundred miles east of Cape Horn, Chile, which Shackleton called "the Gateway to the Antarctic." The island, deserted except for a few whaling stations, was the explorers' last contact with civilization.

Shackleton's crew attempt to carve
a path through treacherous pack ice.

On December 5, the party sailed toward the Weddell Sea,
the southernmost arm of the Atlantic Ocean, and headed for
Antarctica. As Alfred Lansing detailed in his monumental history,
Endurance, published in 1959, Shackleton planned to navigate
through these waters, which were choked with pack ice and
bergs, and establish a base camp on the shore. Then, after waiting
out the winter, he would trek with six men across the continent,
completing the journey at the Ross Sea, a bay that flows into the
Pacific Ocean, south of New Zealand.

On January 18, 1915, barely a hundred miles from the base camp,

BELOW: The ship's wooden hull
groaned in the grip of the ice.

the *Endurance* became encased in sea ice—frozen, as one of the
men put it, "like an almond in the middle of a chocolate bar." The
floe drifted out to sea, carrying the *Endurance* with it, and by late
February, with the onset of winter, Shackleton realized that he
and his party would be imprisoned in the icebound ship until the
November melt.

While they floated through the darkness, Shackleton strove to keep his party united. His methods were considered unorthodox and even radical, at least in the eyes of those accustomed to the mores of the British Navy. He ignored the stifling hierarchies of class and rank, and required that each man receive the same rations and perform the same chores. And though Shackleton sometimes erupted in anger and left no doubt who was in charge—everyone called him the Boss—he participated in menial tasks and mingled easily with his men. A former naval officer on the expedition, writing in his diary, expressed shock that Shackleton "errs on the side of over familiarity and does not rebuke members who occasionally address him with a lack of respect." He said of the Boss, "He is the very reverse of Captain Scott."

To ease the boredom and the dread, Shackleton tried to give the wayward ship a playful atmosphere. The men held regular poker

games, and on Sundays a phonograph wafted music through the berths. Once a month, the men gathered, by lantern, in the dining room—the Ritz, as they called it—to watch Frank Hurley, a photographer who was documenting the expedition, present slides of places around the world that he had visited. The most popular showing was "Peeps in Java," with images of palm trees and maidens from the tropical island. Frank Worsley wrote that Shackleton "appreciated how deeply one man, or small group of men, could affect the psychology of the others," adding that "he almost insisted upon cheeriness and optimism."

But Shackleton was powerless over the ice, and on October 27 the hull's wooden planks began to crack under the pressure. Water burst through the seams, flooding the berths. While the men tried to drain the bilge, the stern of the ship thrust toward the sky, as if in prayer. Shackleton cried, "She's going, boys!"

Everyone quickly lowered the three lifeboats and the provisions onto the surrounding ice, and abandoned the *Endurance*. They were marooned on an ice floe more than a thousand miles southwest of South Georgia Island, with no means of signalling for help. In his diary, Shackleton wrote, "I pray God I can manage to get the whole party safe to civilization."

The waterways were too clogged with pack ice to launch the lifeboats, and so the men trekked on foot, dragging not only the sleds with their supplies but also the lifeboats, which they would need when the ice gave way. Each vessel—the largest was twenty-two-and-a-half feet long and six feet wide—weighed at least a ton, and Shackleton told the men that they must discard any nonessential items. One of Shackleton's most cherished belongings was a Bible given to him by Queen Alexandra, the wife

BELOW: After losing the *Endurance,* Shackleton's
crew tried to drag the lifeboats across the ice.

of Edward VII, which she had inscribed, "May the Lord help you
to do your duty & guide you through all the dangers." Shackleton
laid the Bible on the ice, along with several gold sovereigns.

The other men began to winnow their possessions. Still,
the boats were nearly impossible to haul, and two days later
Shackleton suspended the march. For months, they remained
trapped in tents on the island of ice, which they dubbed Patience
Camp. Frank Worsley wondered "why people had always pictured
Hell as a place that was hot," instead of a realm as "cold as the ice
which seemed likely to become our grave."

To prevent unrest, Shackleton kept three of the most troublesome characters in his own tent. Nevertheless, one day at the end of December, the ship's carpenter, who was in another tent, began to revolt, insisting that, with the *Endurance* lost, the crew was no longer bound to obey its commander. Shackleton summoned the other members of the party, who professed their loyalty to him, and, after the carpenter was left to contemplate the prospect of his survival alone, the mutiny ended.

On April 9, 1916, the ice floe began to crack, and Shackleton gave the long-awaited order: "Launch the boats." After nearly a week, the party reached Elephant Island, a rocky, barren scrap of land a hundred and fifty miles from mainland Antarctica and eight hundred miles southwest of South Georgia Island. Shackleton realized that many of the men could not survive a longer boat journey—one had to have five frostbitten toes amputated—and announced that he would leave most of the group on Elephant Island while he pressed on with five men, including Worsley, in one of the lifeboats.

Amid a hurricane and towering waves glittering with ice, they navigated across the open ocean. The men were soaked and freezing, and Shackleton doled out bits of food from their dwindling rations to keep them conscious. On May 10, nearly a year and a half after departing from South Georgia Island, they stumbled upon its shores again. They looked like the survivors of an apocalypse. Shackleton then took Worsley and another crew

Leaving twenty-two men behind, Shackleton embarks
from Elephant Island with a small party to seek help.

member and trekked north for twenty-six miles, climbing over
uncharted glaciers, to get to a whaling station on the island's
opposite coast, where they could summon help. During the
journey, Shackleton said, he felt a divine presence—a "fourth
man"—guiding them.

When they staggered into the whaling station, thirty-six hours
later, Shackleton immediately turned his attention to rescuing
the twenty-two men stranded on Elephant Island. But it took
him until August 20 to obtain, from the Chilean government,
a steamship big enough to break through the sea ice. As he
approached the island with Worsley, he peered through binoculars

BELOW: The stranded men cheer
Shackleton's return with a relief boat.

to see if anyone was alive. "There are only two," he muttered. "No, four." After a pause, he said, "I see six—*eight*." Then he exclaimed, "They're all there! Every one of them!" Worsley later marvelled at Shackleton's "genius for leadership," which "enabled us to win through when the dice of the elements were loaded most heavily against us." Shackleton later wrote that he and his men, in the course of their journey, had "pierced the veneer of outside things" and "reached the naked soul of man."

But Shackleton had failed in his mission to become the first person to cross the continent, and in 1922 he died of a heart attack,

at the age of forty-seven. His fame soon dimmed, while the grim march to death of his rival, Scott, held the public's imagination. As the historian Max Jones notes in his 2003 book, *The Last Great Quest*, heroes are a reflection of the societies that venerate them. And at a time when Britain's empire was in decline, and the world was grappling with the slaughter of the First World War, Scott was seen as a martyr who had sacrificed himself for his country. By the end of the twentieth century, though, the era of polar exploration was increasingly viewed through the lens of strategy, and Scott was criticized for his imperious, mercurial nature and his inflexible methods. In a 1999 essay, the travel writer Paul Theroux captured this revisionist view: "Scott was insecure, dark, panicky, humorless, an enigma to his men, unprepared, and a bungler."

In an age preoccupied with human mastery—over companies, battlefields, bureaucracies, and, most of all, oneself—Shackleton was revered for the way he had recruited and managed his men, coolly guiding them to safety. His conduct was studied by entrepreneurs, executives, astronauts, scientists, political strategists, and military commanders. An entire subgenre of self-help literature devoted to analyzing his methods emerged, books with titles like *Leading at the Edge: Leadership Lessons from the Extraordinary Saga of Shackleton's Antarctic Expedition*. Another example, *Shackleton: Leadership Lessons from Antarctica*, included such chapters as "Be My Tent Mate: Keep Dissidents Close," "Camaraderie at 20 Below Zero: Creating an Optimal

Work Environment," and "Sailing Uncharted Waters: Adapt and Innovate."

In reducing a man's life to a how-to guide, these books often glossed over some of Shackleton's weaknesses—his almost naïvely ambitious endeavors and his tactical mistakes. They all preached the same gospel: "By Endurance We Conquer." Still, not even a cynic could deny Shackleton's gifts as a commander. As one polar explorer put it, "For scientific leadership, give me Scott; for swift and efficient travel, Amundsen; but when you are in a hopeless situation, when there seems to be no way out, get on your knees and pray for Shackleton."

IV | A SPINE OF STEEL

Henry Worsley on a visit to the Falkland Islands.

WHEN HENRY WORSLEY BEGAN COMMANDING MEN in battle, he tried to emulate Shackleton. Forgoing the privileges of Army rank, Worsley befriended the members of his unit and shared in their tasks. When his soldiers shaved their heads, he cut off his hair, too—even though the look was, as a superior pointed out to him, "rather un-officer-like." Worsley espoused patience and optimism, and tried to demonstrate to his men that, as he put it, "their welfare, and their lives, matter most of all." Nick Carter, who is now Chief of the General Staff, the head of the British Army, said that Worsley had a "very caring and sympathetic attitude to his soldiers—or, as we like to call them, his riflemen." He added, "He was one of those figures who people followed because he was quite an aspirational leader. People would like to *be* him."

Though Worsley generally displayed a modest temperament, he had moments of flamboyance. When he wasn't in uniform, he liked to wear a bright-colored belt or shirt. He kept ferrets as pets and he drove a Harley-Davidson, a cigar often clamped between his teeth. Like Shackleton, who considered poetry "vital mental medicine," he could quote verse by such writers as Robert Browning and Rudyard Kipling. When he was stationed abroad— his initial posting, in 1980, was in Cyprus—he painted the novel landscapes, and when he first faced the threat of violence, in Northern Ireland, he took up sewing to calm his nerves. He could often be seen in his quarters with his needlepoint, at work on a rug or a cushion, before seizing his weapon and heading into the streets. When back in London, he volunteered at a prison to teach tatting—a form of lace-making—to inmates.

In 1988, Worsley, by then promoted to captain, was drawn to the Special Air Service, whose forces, clad in black, had a mystique of unsurpassed fitness and derring-do. Just as there were self-help books on Shackleton's methods, there were manuals on how to master the SAS's "endurance techniques" and "practical leadership" skills, including how to foster a "team mind" and the "will to survive." Worsley signed up for the SAS's selection course, which is so physically punishing that participants have died trying to pass it. In 2013, two men on a prolonged trek fatally collapsed from heat exhaustion; a third was rushed to the hospital, and later died of organ failure. (According to legend, after two candidates lost their lives during a test in 1981, the chief instructor remarked, "Death is Nature's way of telling you you've failed.")

The course lasted six months, and during its first stage Worsley had to complete a series of timed marches—known as "death marches"—through the Brecon Beacons, a mountain range in South Wales. He trekked for days in full combat gear, consuming little more than water and carrying a heavy rucksack. He could see other applicants collapsing and quitting; their minds often gave out before their bodies. The marches culminated in what was known as the Endurance—a forty-mile hike, over a three-thousand-foot-high peak, that he had to finish in less than twenty-two hours while carrying a fifty-five-pound rucksack.

After completing this part of the course, he was flown to Brunei, where he was helicoptered into a jungle filled with orangutans and cloud leopards and poisonous snakes. He had to survive for a week while eluding a band of soldiers tasked with hunting him down. The administrators of the course had eyes on the ground to observe him—to see what kind of clay he was made of. Later, he was subjected to an interrogation intended to break him. "You are beaten up," one applicant told a reporter, noting that any vulnerability was exploited: "If you've got a phobia about

spiders, they'll use it against you." Each year, only about fifteen
percent of applicants pass the selection course. Worsley was among
them. An SAS officer close to Worsley said that his "gentle, artistic
side could mask a very significant spine of steel." Worsley went
on to serve two tours with the SAS, a rare distinction for a junior
officer.

ONE EVENING AT A PARTY IN LONDON IN 1989, WORSLEY
met Joanna Stainton. Whereas he often stood back warily in social
settings, Joanna, a tall, graceful woman with auburn hair, moved
with ease. She had worked for a time in Los Angeles, producing
music videos for MTV. Though she liked to travel, she hated
camping and the wintry cold, and she especially hated ferrets. Still,
she and Worsley began dating. "Talk about opposites attracting,"
she said. "Christ, I'm a complete pavement girl."

Yet she loved the way that Worsley seemed to come from a
bygone age—"a man out of his time," as a relative once described
him—believing unabashedly in ideals of courage and sacrifice.
She loved his eccentric hobbies, and how he recited poetry to
her and held her with arms that seemed unbreakable. He loved
her brashness and her ability to talk to anyone, whether at an
art benefit or at a homeless shelter, where she often volunteered.
And he loved the way she punctured his stoicism and exposed
his hidden self, always urging him to "go out and achieve your

dreams." For all her free-spiritedness, she was the steadiest presence in his life. He called her his "rock."

They married in 1993. Max was born the following year, and Alicia in 1996. Nick Carter said, "Worsley lusted after adventure but also relished being at home with his family—teaching his son to shoot or to ferret, or simply cutting wood for the winter and cutting the grass." Because of his military postings, though, Worsley was often separated from his family, as his father had been. In 2001, he was serving in Bosnia when a riot broke out in the streets. A civilian was beaten to death, and crowds began to chase Worsley. As he recounted in his book, he sought refuge in a café, but the crowds closed in, throwing stones and smashing the windows. "How would Shacks get out of this, then?" he asked himself. He knew that if he remained in the café, the situation would only worsen: "I had to be decisive and make a move, as Shackleton had done." He pinpointed a place in the distance where he could find cover, and he made a break for it, dashing through the onslaught and summoning his regiment. He then defused the uprising by deploying his soldiers around the area and persuading the ringleaders to back down—using what Carter later described as "a very subtle use of coercion and negotiation." In 2002, Worsley was awarded the Queen's Commendation for Valuable Service, in "recognition of gallant and distinguished services."

Many officers and soldiers admired him the way he admired

Shackleton. Carter described him to a reporter as "one of the most understated but bravest people I have known," and a soldier who had served under Worsley hailed him as a "fiercely capable leader of men." Yet his military career soon stalled. Joanna recalled, "He loved the soldiering part of soldiering, but once you command your regiment, at about the age of forty, all the postings after that

are slightly more political desk-type jobs, which Henry hated." A former officer said that Worsley refused to jockey for position, noting, "That wasn't his style." Worsley, who had been promoted to lieutenant colonel in 2000, watched as many of his closest friends were becoming brigadiers and generals.

His fascination with Shackleton, meanwhile, seemed to deepen. He spent hours at antique shops and auction houses, in search of what he called Shackletonia: autographed books and photographs and diaries and correspondence and other memorabilia. "Henry lost a fortune on it all," Joanna recalled. At one auction, he bid feverishly

on a first edition of Shackleton's book about the *Endurance*
expedition, *South,* in which Shackleton had inscribed a message
to his parents: "With Love from Ernest, Xmas 1919." Every time
Worsley made an offer, a person bidding anonymously over the
telephone countered him and finally made off with the prize, at a
price of seven thousand dollars. Weeks later, on his tenth wedding
anniversary, Joanna gave him a present: the inscribed book.
Each had been unaware that the other was the rival bidder. He
considered the gift to be his "most treasured possession of all."

In November of 2003, he made a pilgrimage to a place that he
had dreamed of visiting since he was a boy: South Georgia Island.
Not only had Shackleton and Frank Worsley found refuge there
after the sinking of the *Endurance;* the two men also had returned
to the island in 1922, preparing for a new Antarctic expedition.
The day after their arrival, Shackleton had suffered his heart attack
and died. ("His stillness was startling to me, for stillness was
the one thing that I found it impossible to associate with him,"
Frank Worsley wrote.) After Frank Worsley and other members
of the expedition buried Shackleton, at a cemetery on the island,
they found stones and built a cairn to mark the grave. And as
they raised this makeshift memorial, Frank Worsley recalled, "a
snowstorm beat down upon us—a ghost, it seemed to me, of the
hurricane in which he and I had approached South Georgia after
our boat journey from Elephant Island."

More than eighty years later, Henry Worsley, carrying a

rucksack and a sleeping bag, pried open the cemetery gate and went inside. It was twilight, and he could just make out the cairn and a granite tombstone, which was engraved with a paraphrase of a line by Robert Browning: "I hold that a man should strive to the uttermost for his life's set prize." Worsley put his sleeping bag on the ground and climbed inside it, facing the block of granite. "Reaching out to touch it I considered for a moment just how significant a moment in my life this was," he later wrote, adding, "I was about to spend the night . . . beside the grave of my hero since childhood."

Afterward, he found a sonnet, by an explorer from New Zealand named Hugh de Lautour, which echoed his feelings so intensely that he annotated it and often recited it aloud:

Rest, Sir Ernest, rest beneath your star;
All striving done and "life's set prize" attained:
Not geographic goals, but greater far
The pinnacles of leadership you gained.
Rest, Sir Ernest, rest. God knows there's none
Deserves it more: the long Antarctic night
Now friend, not foe, with South's white warfare won
And crew from death's dark door led back to light.
How was it your endurance overcame
The daily struggle just to keep alive
Long past the point where death would bring no shame?

BELOW: In 2003, Worsley visited Shackleton's
grave on South Georgia Island.

Half starved and frozen, how did you survive,
And how was no man lost while in your care?
God knows. God knows it well. For He was there.

After his trip to South Georgia, Worsley longed even more to
make his own polar journey, to obtain his own "life's set prize," but
he doubted that he ever would. As he put it, "I was afraid of the
unknown—the planning, the training, the fund-raising and, not
least, the risk of failure."

V | PLAN OF ATTACK

ONE DAY IN MARCH 2004, WORSLEY WAS CONTACTED by Alexandra Shackleton, the explorer's granddaughter. He'd met her several years earlier, at Christie's in London, when he had successfully bid on an autographed photograph of her grandfather. Afterward, Worsley periodically ran into her at lectures on polar exploration, and he had shared with her his desire to make an Antarctic expedition.

Alexandra told Worsley that she wanted him to meet another Shackleton descendant—a great-nephew—named Will Gow.

"Like you, he admires my grandfather very much and for a few years now has had an idea for an expedition," she said.

At a pub in South London, Worsley met with Gow, a thirty-three-year-old banker with a pudgy face and squinty blue eyes that widened in moments of excitement. Gow eagerly explained that the centennial of the *Nimrod* expedition was a few years away, and that when the anniversary arrived he wanted to reenact the journey. Worsley was steeped in the details of the failed journey. On October 29, 1908, Shackleton had departed for the South Pole with three other men, including a meteorologist named Jameson Boyd Adams, who was his second-in-command. After coming within ninety-seven nautical miles of the Pole, on January 9, 1909, Shackleton planted a British flag in the ice, taking, in his words, "possession of this plateau in the name of His Majesty King Edward the Seventh." He then faced a terrible quandary: he knew that he could reach the Pole in several days, capturing the grail, but if he kept going he would deplete the food the party needed for the return journey and jeopardize the lives of his men, who were already fading. Ultimately, Shackleton made what Worsley considered "the most selfless and astonishing decision ever in the history of polar exploration"—he turned back.

Gow envisaged that the new expedition would be composed of descendants of men who had explored alongside Shackleton. They would try to reach Shackleton's farthest point on

January 9, 2009—exactly a hundred years after he did—and then press on to the South Pole, completing, in Gow's words, "unfinished family business."

Worsley listened in amazement. Here was the chance of a lifetime. He was confident that the Army would grant him a leave for the expedition. And so, like two conspirators, Worsley and Gow began plotting their journey. They needed to find another recruit and to raise four hundred thousand dollars to cover the costs of equipment and travel. And they needed to train: though they had polar exploration in their genes, they had no actual experience.

They began a ruthless exercise regimen. Each tied tractor tires to a harness around his waist, and then dragged them back and forth across an open field. In 2005, they signed up for the Montane Yukon Arctic Ultra, a race through the icy wilderness of northwest Canada, which is billed as the toughest endurance competition in the world. Temperatures can fall to minus fifty degrees, and participants have had toes and fingers amputated because of frostbite. *Newsweek* once observed that the event—which scientists have used to study the impact of extreme conditions on the human body—sounded like the "premise for a Jack London novel."

There were different categories for the race, and Worsley and Gow entered one that required them to trek on foot for three hundred miles—a third of the distance of their planned South Pole journey—while hauling all their supplies on sleds. They

Will Gow and Worsley train
for the South Pole expedition.

had eight days to complete the race. "Beyond coping with the physical demands, I wanted to see if I had the mental strength," Worsley wrote, adding, "Any sign of quitting on this short event would spell disaster for the future challenge and, if I did give up . . . I would have to seriously consider my place in the expedition team."

Armed with flares and swaddled in layers of clothing, they dragged their sleds through dense pine forests and over mountains and across frozen rivers, where Gow's foot once broke through the ice and into the water. They had been told that if they got wet they had only about five minutes to prevent hypothermia, and Gow quickly lit a fire, dried his foot, and changed his clothing. Onward the men went. Above them, the northern lights cast a haunting green glow.

After several days of trekking, Worsley and Gow suffered from sleeplessness and sensory deprivation, and they grew dizzy from hunger. Soon, they began to hallucinate. To keep going, Worsley resorted to "drastic measures," imagining that he was pulling his sick daughter on the sled and had to get her to the doctor if she were to live. He and Gow slumped across the finish line, beating the time limit by several hours. "That was really the first test," Gow recalled.

IN 2006, TWO YEARS BEFORE THE PLANNED EXPEDITION, Worsley was dispatched to Helmand Province, in Afghanistan, to provide "eyes and ears," as he put it, before British forces were deployed to the region. He took with him his dog-eared copy of *The Heart of the Antarctic*, Shackleton's account of the *Nimrod* expedition; paints and brushes and a sewing kit; and a bag of cricket bats and balls, to play with the locals. For months, he travelled across Helmand, conferring with tribal elders and mullahs. Worsley later wrote in an article, "Surviving in Afghanistan was as much about an empathy with the people and their culture as it was about troop numbers and firepower."

After gathering intelligence, he warned his superiors that the arrival of British forces risked "stirring up a hornets' nest" by agitating the population and provoking violent reprisals from the Taliban. His words were prophetic. "Henry, rightly, foresaw the trouble that was to come," Tom Tugendhat, a member of the British Parliament, later told a reporter. But, at the time, Worsley's alarms rankled many military and political leaders who were downplaying the dangers to the public, and, if Worsley had any remaining hope of military advancement, his candor ended it. Yet he was no longer disappointed. In a commonplace book, he jotted

BELOW: Henry Adams's great-grandfather
Jameson Boyd Adams.

down the advice Shackleton had given after the sinking of the
Endurance: "A man must shape himself to a new mark directly the
old one goes to ground." And it occurred to Worsley that had he
been promoted he would not have had the time to prepare for the
upcoming expedition and become the explorer that he had always
wanted to be. "He suddenly realized that he could fulfill some
dreams," Joanna recalled.

By the time Worsley returned from Afghanistan, Gow had
found a third recruit: Henry Adams, a thirty-two-year-old
shipping lawyer. Adams seemed a bit pale and spindly for an
explorer, but he had a genial personality, and he was deeply
committed. What's more, he was the great-grandson of Jameson

Boyd Adams, the second-in-command on
the *Nimrod* expedition.

That April, Worsley and his two
companions headed to Baffin Island, a
Canadian territory nine hundred miles west
of Greenland. For several weeks, they trained
with Matty McNair, a fifty-four-year-old
American explorer, who, in 1997, had led the
first all-female expedition to the North Pole.
This was the men's longest exposure yet to
polar conditions, and they made embarrassing
blunders. They forgot to turn off a portable
stove, and nearly engulfed their tent in flames.

TOP: Gow's great-uncle Ernest Shackleton.
BOTTOM: Henry Worsley's ancestor Frank Worsley.

They skied too slowly and never seemed to navigate along a straight line. One day, after Worsley declined to wear tinted goggles, he suffered from snow blindness. But he and the others learned from their mistakes, and emerged with a better understanding, as Adams put it, of how "to live on the ice."

The trip, however, had brought to a head a simmering problem: the team's lack of clear leadership. Gow was ostensibly in charge, but the expedition was plagued by disorganization, causing tension among the men; moreover, only a fraction of the necessary funds had been raised. In their tent on Baffin Island, Worsley broached the matter with Gow, threatening to drop out of the expedition if things didn't change. "Henry didn't dodge bullets," Adams recalled. After some consideration, Gow asked Worsley to take charge. "With his military background, it made very good sense," Gow recalled. "Adams and myself were young whippersnappers. We were quite happy to have some wise old owl leading us away."

58

Gow, Worsley, and Adams
training in Greenland.

In the two years before their
departure, Worsley was consumed
with the mission. Late at night, after
completing his Army duties, he wrote
letters seeking meetings with potential
donors. "If he got his foot in the
door, he would usually come out with
money," his son, Max, recalled. "His
passion and his fire—you could see it
within him. It gripped people."

Like a general developing a plan
of attack, Worsley spent hours poring
over maps, laying out a precise route
for the expedition. The more he studied
Antarctica, the more forbidding it
seemed. The continent is nearly five and
a half million square miles—larger than Europe—and it doubles in
size in winter, when its coastal waters freeze over. Approximately
ninety-eight percent of Antarctica is covered in an ice sheet, which
rises and drops and bends over the varied topography. The sheet—
which, in places, is fifteen thousand feet thick—contains about
seventy percent of the freshwater, and ninety percent of the
ice, on Earth.

Yet Antarctica is classified as a desert, because there is so
little precipitation. It is the driest and highest continent, with

BELOW: Camped on an iceberg
off the Greenland coast.

an average elevation of seventy-five hundred feet. It is also the windiest, with gusts reaching up to two hundred miles per hour, and the coldest, with temperatures in the interior falling below minus seventy-five degrees. (Scientists have used the Antarctic to test spacesuits for Mars, where the average surface temperature is minus sixty-seven.)

Worsley, Gow, and Adams planned to begin their journey south of New Zealand, on Ross Island. The island is bound by the Ross Ice Shelf, which extends over the Ross Sea and is the largest body of floating ice in the world—more than a hundred and eighty thousand square miles and, on average, more than a thousand feet

thick. Because the Ross Ice Shelf is easier to reach by sea during the summer than other parts of the continent, and because it is relatively smooth and stretches nearly six hundred miles toward the heart of Antarctica, it was the starting point for expeditions to the South Pole during the golden age of Antarctic exploration. Shackleton and Scott and Amundsen all began their expeditions on the shelf.

Like these explorers, Worsley and his team would head south across the ice shelf, a journey of nearly four hundred nautical miles, until they reached the Transantarctic Mountains, which divide the continent and extend to the Weddell Sea. To get to the Polar Plateau—an elevated, almost featureless part of the continental ice shelf, where the South Pole is situated—the party would have to cross these mountains, which rise nearly fifteen thousand feet. On the *Nimrod* expedition, Shackleton discovered one of the few passable routes: a glacier-covered valley, twenty-five miles wide and a hundred and twenty-five miles long, that runs between the mountains like a frozen causeway. "There burst upon our vision an open road to the South," Shackleton wrote.

Still, the glacier—which Shackleton named Beardmore, after William Beardmore, a Scottish industrialist and a patron of his expedition—is treacherous. Its elevation is eight thousand feet, and its surface is riddled with crevasses. The last of Shackleton's Manchurian ponies had disappeared into one. When Scott crossed the glacier during his later expedition, one of his men suffered a fatal head injury after falling into a crevasse. Only a dozen people—the same number that have walked on the Moon—had trekked the length of the glacier. Worsley referred to it as his "nemesis."

If he and his companions survived the crossing, they would emerge on the Polar Plateau, where they would ascend the ten-thousand-foot-high Titan Dome to reach Shackleton's farthest point: 88°23′S, 162°E. Finally, Worsley's party would trek the remaining ninety-seven nautical miles to the Pole, whose elevation is ninety-three hundred feet.

"Every spare hour was devoted to the project and 'bloody Shackleton' became a phrase frequently used by the children," Worsley wrote. By October of 2008, he and his colleagues were ready to embark on what had been officially named the Matrix Shackleton Centenary Expedition. Before leaving, Worsley and his family gathered for an early Christmas celebration. Even though Henry had been telling Joanna for years about the glories of Antarctica, it still seemed to her like the most dreadful place in the world. Yet she believed that, to borrow Thomas Pynchon's words, "Everyone has an Antarctic"—someplace people seek to find answers about themselves. In the case of her husband, it was the Antarctic itself. And so she gave her blessing to the adventure, even though it threatened to take from her the man she loved.

The Beardmore Glacier. Worsley called it his "nemesis."

Alicia and Max painted their father's skis with messages. One quoted Shackleton's family motto: "By Endurance We Conquer."

Worsley's decision was harder for his children to understand. Alicia, who was twelve, saw his sled primarily as an object to play on. When the family exchanged Christmas gifts, Max, who was fourteen, seemed agitated. This was different from when his father was deployed by the military—Worsley had not had a choice then about leaving them behind. This was a response to some mysterious inner calling. Max had written a poem about Antarctica, a place that now loomed in his own imagination, and he composed a short essay about his father's upcoming journey. "I have heard many stories about Shackleton since I was very young and as I grew older, I started to understand and admire Shackleton more," he wrote. "I am very happy for my Dad that he is doing what he has always wanted to do, but I am also worried for him. Even in the most barren place in the world there is a risk of falling down a glacier or crevasse."

Joanna drove her husband to the airport, where she began to cry. He told her not to worry, and quoted Shackleton: "Better a live donkey than a dead lion."

VI | GET WET AND YOU DIE

O N OCTOBER 30, 2008, WORSLEY, GOW, AND ADAMS arrived in Punta Arenas, on the southern tip of Chile. They went to a warehouse owned by a company named Antarctic Logistics & Expeditions. During the summer, between thirty thousand and forty-five thousand tourists visit the continent, nearly all of them travelling on small cruise ships. Worsley's party had hired ALE to provide logistical support, which included transporting them by airplane to their starting point on Ross Island.

At the warehouse, Worsley and his companions collected freeze-dried meals for the expedition. They faced the same predicament that had bedevilled polar explorers for generations: they could haul only so many supplies on their sleds, a situation that left them vulnerable to starvation. Shackleton, during the *Nimrod* expedition, wrote ruefully, "How one wishes for time and unlimited provisions. Then indeed we could penetrate the secrets of this great lonely continent."

Worsley estimated that the journey would take nine weeks. Each of the men would be limited to about three hundred and ten pounds of provisions, including a sled, and so they whittled down their kit to the essentials. Worsley packed his portion of the food, which was sealed in ten bags—one for each week of the journey, plus an extra in case of emergency. His clothing included two pairs of pants, a fleece shirt, a down jacket with a hood, gloves, a neck gaiter, a face mask, two pairs of long johns, and three pairs of socks. He brought cross-country skis and poles; for climbing, he carried crampons and ropes. As the only member of the team with first-aid training, he transported the medical bag, which contained antibiotics, syringes, splints, and morphine. He made room for his diary and a copy of *The Heart of the Antarctic*. And he carefully stored what he considered the most vital piece of equipment: a satellite phone with solar-powered batteries, which would allow the men not only to record short audio dispatches but also to check in every day with an ALE operator and report their coordinates and medical condition. If the team failed to communicate for two consecutive days, ALE would dispatch a search-and-rescue plane—what Worsley called "the most expensive taxi ride in the world."

The men permitted themselves the luxury of iPods, as well as a deck of cards and a few mementos. Worsley carried an envelope filled with notes from family and friends, which Joanna had given him to open when he needed encouragement. In his front pocket, he had tucked away one more precious object: the brass compass that Shackleton used on his expedition. Alexandra Shackleton had asked Worsley to bring it with him, hoping that, this time, it would reach the South Pole.

For Worsley, getting closer to Shackleton was a way of getting closer to himself. During an interview with an exploration website, he outlined the qualities that he most admired in Shackleton, including his "optimism and patience," his "courage," and his ability, when his men's lives were at stake, to instill in them the "confidence that he would get them out of the desperate situation."

Commanding the expedition was far trickier than commanding soldiers in the military. In Antarctica, his authority was not official but merely granted, and he had no more experience as a polar explorer than his peers did. Yet he felt the immeasurable weight of being responsible for their lives. He now formed a pact with Gow and Adams: "There would be no egos, no pride and if someone was feeling unwell or traveling slowly, then he should have no difficulty in accepting the offer from one of the others to carry some of his weight."

On November 10, the ALE plane was ready for departure. After decades of dreaming, Worsley's Antarctic journey was beginning.

THE PLANE—AN ENORMOUS SOVIET-DESIGNED FREIGHTER, which was so loud that Worsley and the others could barely hear their own voices—took them to an ALE camp on the side of Antarctica that is south of Cape Horn, a flight of four and a half hours. On arrival, they skidded onto a runway of ice. After waiting for the weather to clear, they boarded a smaller, twin-propeller aircraft with landing skis. As they flew across the continent, they peered out the window at deep gashes in the ice sheet below. "Everywhere we looked, there were crevasse fields the size of a small parish," Worsley wrote. "What we were about to undertake was brought sharply into focus in those few moments. None of us said a word." Finally, after flying eleven hours and more than twelve hundred miles to the southwest, the plane touched down on the sea ice by Ross Island. "My God, we've made it," Worsley exclaimed.

For years, he had been constructing Antarctica in his mind, and after climbing down from the plane he joyously stamped his boots on three-foot-thick ice. The temperature was about minus fourteen

degrees, and his nostrils burned. It was late in the afternoon, but
because it was summer the sun remained bright, and he could see
two of the volcanoes on Ross Island that had been beacons for
polar explorers: Mount Terror, which is more than ten thousand

feet high, and dormant, and
Mount Erebus, an active
volcano, which is more than
twelve thousand feet high.
Black smoke drifted from its
icy cone.

Not far from the men,
penguins slid on their bellies
across the ice—the world
not yet deadened. And
on the southern tip of the
island, about twenty-two
miles away, was McMurdo
Station, which was opened
by the U.S. government in
1955 and has served since
then as a hub for scientific
research. In the summer,
around a thousand people
live at the base, the largest
population in Antarctica.

With its power station and its dormitories carved into the ice, the base has the look of a grimy truck stop.

The men headed onto the island. As they climbed a ridge overlooking a bowl-shaped valley, Worsley came to an abrupt halt. Down below, amid volcanic rock and ice, was a solitary wooden hut with shuttered windows and an iron chimney. Worsley didn't need to say what it was. They all knew. It was the hut that

Shackleton and his party had built in February 1908 and stayed in that winter, before setting out for the South Pole. Shackleton had called the shelter "the Mecca of all our hopes and dreams." In 2004, a team of conservationists had begun restoring the hut, and to Worsley it looked just as it had in the grainy photograph in *The Heart of the Antarctic.*

Gow raced over and opened the door, and Worsley and Adams followed him inside. In the dimness, Worsley could discern the scattered debris of the *Nimrod* expedition, as if the party had momentarily stepped away. There were canned goods, leather boots with frayed laces, and blue bottles of medicine marked DIARRHEA. Two sleds were suspended in the rafters, and hanging on a wall was a framed photograph of Queen Alexandra. Shackleton, in his diary, had described a shaft of light passing over the image before they set out on their trek, which he had deemed "an omen of good luck."

Gow gasped at the ghostly scene. Adams found the bunk where his great-grandfather had slept, while Worsley examined the dark recesses of the room as if he were rummaging through a tomb. "I could hardly get closer to my mentor," he later wrote. "The only thing left to do was to walk in his footsteps to the Pole."

That night, the men camped inside the hut, lying on the frozen ground in their sleeping bags. The silence among them betrayed their nerves. The next morning, November 14, Worsley was the first to get up. "It had been impossible to sleep," he noted. "The

After visiting Shackleton's hut, Worsley wrote, "The only thing left to do was to walk in his footsteps to the Pole."

enormity of the task seemed overwhelming." He put on his boots, slipped outside the tent, and called the ALE operator. "The Matrix Shackleton Expedition calling in with our first report," he said. "We are setting off in a couple hours. All is well. No medical problems."

"OK," the operator replied. "Have a great journey."

Worsley's companions had awakened, and the three men began

mummifying themselves in layers of clothing and loading their provisions onto their sleds. Worsley made sure to distribute the weight evenly on his sled, and he covered his cargo with a tarp. The sled—which was emblazoned with the words "Always a little further" and "By Endurance We Conquer"— resembled a torpedo. After attaching the sled to a harness around his waist, Worsley clipped his boots into his skis, seeing the messages that his family had painted on them: "Don't give up," "Push it, fat ass."

At 10 A.M.—the hour that Shackleton had set out—Worsley and his men leaned into their harnesses and began their trek. This was the moment that he'd been waiting for nearly all his life, Worsley thought. Yet, as he strained with his arms and his legs to propel himself forward and drag the heavy sled, he was gnawed by doubts: "I was nervous about lots of things; of failing the team; of getting injured; of letting down all those people who had supported us; of plainly not being physically up for it—put simply, I feared failure."

The surface was generally flat and smooth, and as he and the other men headed south, toward the Ross Ice Shelf, they began to gather some momentum. Worsley made sure that they followed the advice of Matty McNair, who had instructed them on Baffin Island: "Stay together, never separate." She had drummed into them one other rule: "If you get wet, you die."

Worsley, Gow, and Adams, near the start of their journey.

After several miles, they came upon another desolate wooden hut. Robert Falcon Scott and his men had built it in 1911, on their fateful South Pole expedition. Ice crept over the timbered walls and glazed the windowpanes like jungle vines. Inside the hut, Worsley and his companions found the chart table where Scott had studied his maps, and the bunk belonging to Captain Lawrence Oates, who had left the party's tent on the return journey from the Pole, saying, "I am just going outside and may be some time." He was never seen again.

As Worsley inspected the objects, he felt uneasy: "I couldn't shake the sense of pathetic sadness from my mind." The men quickly resumed tracing the path of their forebears, which had long since been obliterated by the windswept ice. The fresh tracks made by Worsley and his companions gradually vanished as well; tiny granules of ice swirled in the wind like ash. The men used a compass to maintain a southward trajectory. Their breath smoked and their bodies sweated in the arid cold. After slogging for seven hours, Worsley gave the order to stop for the day. They had covered nearly eight nautical miles. In order to reach the ninety-seven-mile mark on January 9, the men would need to average between ten and twelve nautical miles per day. But it was a promising start.

They began the cumbersome process of making camp: pitching their tent, which was roughly fourteen feet long and seven feet wide; gathering provisions from the sled; squeezing inside the shelter and removing their ski boots and sweaty socks, which they

Parked amid a sea of ice.

hung on a clothesline above their heads, along with any other damp items; checking their bodies for frostbite and putting on dry socks and tent "booties"; and firing up a gas cooker, melting snow in a kettle, and pouring hot water into packets of freeze-dried meals.

As the men ate, they talked about the relatively warm weather—the temperature had reached fourteen degrees. Adams

The view from within.

delivered the evening broadcast, reporting that they had been blessed with "beautiful sunshine, exactly as Shackleton had a hundred years ago on his first day." Privately, though, Adams confessed to Worsley and Gow that he felt like an amateur hauling his sled, and had a deep sense of unease. "He was right and honest," Worsley wrote. "None of us knew what the next two months were going to be like."

Following supper, the men dipped their toothbrushes in the snow and cleaned their teeth, which Worsley believed was essential to maintaining a sense of humanity. Then, jostling for space, they spread out their sleeping bags. Worsley, however, didn't climb into his. In spite of his aching muscles and the dropping temperature—the sun was now hugging the horizon—he went for an evening walk. He decided to make this a daily ritual, like a mystic who pursues enlightenment through self-abnegation. The harsh reality of Antarctica had seemed only to deepen his entrancement with it. Outside, he often picked up objects—a fragment of a penguin skull, a small rock—and put them in a pocket, despite the extra weight. "We used to take the Mickey out of him for taking all this rubbish," Gow recalled.

After Worsley's stroll, which lasted about twenty minutes, he returned to the tent and settled into his sleeping bag. They all kept plastic bottles nearby, in case they had to respond to what Adams referred to as a "call of nature." Before falling asleep, Worsley wrote briefly in his diary, ending with a quote from Shackleton: "I pray that we may be successful, for my heart had been so much in this."

Within eight days, they had covered more than seventy-five nautical miles. The scale of the Ross Ice Shelf was dawning on Worsley: it was bigger than France. Shackleton described it as a "dead, smooth, white plain, weird beyond description." Worsley and his men moved in single file and rarely spoke, hearing only the thumping of their sleds or the soundtracks on their iPods. Adams loved to listen to Rachmaninoff's Vespers; Gow sometimes trudged along to an audiobook of Lansing's *Endurance*. Worsley's playlist included Bruce Springsteen and the Seeger Sessions

Band playing "Eyes on the Prize" ("I got my hand on the gospel plow / Won't take nothing for my journey now") and "We Shall Overcome" ("We are not afraid, we are not afraid").

With nothing to stare at but ice, Worsley was becoming a connoisseur of its varieties. It could be squeaky or powdery or crusty. The wind often sculpted it into waves, known as sastrugi, which rose as high as four feet and sometimes extended, in parallel rows, to the horizon. (Adams noted, in a broadcast, that each of the men had his own strategy for traversing the frozen waves: "Henry tends to herringbone over it, Will declares war on the sastrugi, and I tend to try and run at it.") Then, there was the deep, sludgy ice, the most wretched of all, which made them feel like they were plowing through wet sand. Because it was more taxing to be up front, breaking track, the men took hourly turns in the lead.

They were burning between six thousand and eight thousand calories a day, and periodically paused to consume energy drinks and snack on such fatty foods as salami, nuts, and chocolate; even so, they began to lose weight. Worsley, knowing that it was imperative to maintain positive thoughts, recalled family holidays and planting vegetables in the garden. He grew accustomed to the paradox of being reduced to irrelevance in the alien landscape while at the same time feeling acutely aware of oneself: every aching muscle, every joint, every breath, every heartbeat. He said that he preferred breaking track, despite its difficulties, because all you saw in front of you was "the infinite beyond."

Each man devised his own technique
for coping with the wind-sculpted sastrugi.

BELOW: "Stay together, never separate"
was the men's mantra.

One day, Adams spotted in the distance something poking from the ice and gleaming in the blinding sun. "What's that?" he asked.

"No idea," Worsley said.

When they reached it, they realized that it was a meteorological

instrument recording such data as temperature and wind speed. A sign indicated that the device belonged to the University of Wisconsin. The men quickly moved on, but for hours Worsley fumed, resenting the intrusion, and he was relieved when he finally glanced back and the instrument had disappeared from view. As he put it, "We were back on an unblemished canvas."

THE STORM CAME UPON THE MEN SUDDENLY. THE temperature was minus twenty-two degrees, and frigid winds whipped up ice that stung the eyes like bits of glass. It was November 28, 2008, and Worsley's team was two weeks into its journey. The men bent forward, but the wind overwhelmed them, and Worsley concluded that they needed to stop for the day. Moments after they unpacked the tent, the wind nearly hurled it into the white oblivion. They fastened its corners with ice screws and buried the flaps under the snow and used their sleds as barricades. Then the men scurried inside, crouching together and shivering as the tent's nylon fabric rattled.

Worsley called the ALE operator to give their coordinates. "We are caught in a storm and won't be moving today," he said.

"I can hear the wind," the operator replied.

The tempest intensified, the wind hissing at fifty miles per hour. Ice drifted over the tent. "It was as if the elements were furious that we were there," Worsley wrote. When they awoke the

88

Whiteout: "It was as if the elements were
furious that we were there," Worsley wrote.

next day, the storm was even angrier. In a broadcast, Adams said,
"We are tent-bound again." They knew that in 1912, less than ten
nautical miles from their position, Robert Falcon Scott and his
party had died during their trek back from the Pole. "It's a very,
very sobering thought for us," Adams added.

The tent was virtually submerged under ice, and inside, the
air reeked of unwashed bodies and dirty socks and stove fuel.
Worsley—whom Gow and Adams now called the General—tried

89

BELOW: "I pray that we may be successful,"
Worsley wrote in his diary.

to foster a lighthearted atmosphere. The men passed the time
chatting and reading and playing poker. They had previously named
themselves the founding members of the Antarctic Malt Whiskey
Appreciation Society; per its bylaws, every Thursday evening the
explorers would drink from a flask of whiskey, which Gow had
brought with him, and the next morning they would sleep in an
extra two hours. Even though it was a Saturday, the men passed
around the flask. The liquor warmed them. Worsley, who, in the
Army, had honed a gallows humor, joked about their circumstances:
if they could make fun of dying, they still had some life in them.
In an earlier audio broadcast, Worsley had reported, "Morale's
high," adding, "We've just had supper. Will is picking his toes and
Henry Adams is writing in his diary. We'll send you another report
tomorrow. Until then, farewell from the Ross Ice Shelf."

After two more days, the
storm relented. The men
unzipped the tent and began
hacking through a wall of ice
about five feet tall and four
feet thick. They dug for more
than an hour, until they
emerged into the blinding
light, like escaped prisoners.
They packed and pressed on,
trying to make up time.

On a clear day, they could now discern the peaks of the Transantarctic Mountains—"high points piercing the horizon line," as Worsley reported in a broadcast. By the fourth week of their journey, in mid-December, they had made it across the Ross Ice Shelf, to the base of the mountain range. The terrain began to rise, and the surface was scarred with deep fissures, a product of the eternal churning of ice. "All this disturbance meant only one thing—the threat of crevasses," Worsley wrote.

The following day, despite the danger, Worsley went on his walkabout, and collected several rock specimens. Hoping to do reconnaissance for the upcoming route, he continued walking for hours, at one point climbing onto a ledge and looking south. Before him, shrouded in mist, rose the Beardmore Glacier. "I gazed into the gloom wondering just what my nemesis had in store for us," he wrote.

By the time he returned to the tent, it was late, and Adams said, "Ah, General, we were beginning to think you'd met an unfortunate end."

The men gathered their belongings and trekked to the mouth of the glacier. As Adams looked up, he felt that he was confronting a "biblical terror." Every way they turned, it seemed, there was a new obstacle: a boulder of ice, or a towering slope resembling a frozen waterfall, or a snow bridge extending over a crevasse. Some of the crevasses were "wide enough to swallow a car," as Worsley put it. Others were only a few feet deep, but that was enough for

BELOW: Burning between six thousand and eight thousand calories a day, the men couldn't maintain their weight.

someone to break an ankle or twist a knee. If one of the men were injured, there would be no place for miles for a rescue plane to land. An ALE doctor had warned them, "You either get yourself out or you don't get out."

Worsley decided that they could no longer proceed on skis, and so they attached crampons to their boots and put on climbing harnesses, double-checking the screws, slings, and carabiners. Then the men roped themselves together: Worsley in front, followed by Gow and Adams. As they inched up the glacier, their sleds felt like ship anchors being dragged across an ocean floor.

The days were slow and draining. Before each step, Worsley, who was responsible for finding a path, poked his pole in front

of him, to see if the ice was solid. Whenever a hole opened, he leaned over and glimpsed the underworld—a chute swirling into darkness. "The Antarctic can take your life in one of two ways," he noted. "It can wear you down over a prolonged period of time through starvation, cold, and exhaustion, often in the face of appalling weather. Or it can take you into the throat of a crevasse in a split second." Once, Worsley went to retrieve his sleeping bag from his sled after a day of climbing, and the ice cracked open under his right foot. His leg plunged into the shaft. Adams raced over and yanked him out. Each time you escaped, Worsley wrote, "you sensed your luck was running out."

Soon, the men encountered something startling beneath their feet: a sheet of blue ice. The result of snow accumulating on a glacier and being compressed over thousands of years, this kind of ice is so dense—so devoid of air bubbles—that it absorbs long-wavelength light, which is why it appears mesmerizingly blue. Yet, as the men quickly discovered, its beauty is deceptive. "It's hard like concrete," Gow recalled. "Harder than concrete—literally indescribable how hard."

Before long, the aluminum spikes of the crampons began to bend and break. The men slipped again and again, their bodies smacking against the ice, their sleds pulling them downhill. "It was agony," Worsley wrote. "I felt every ridge of ice as I was dragged over its vicious surface." Bruised and bleeding, the men cursed into the wind. "Beardmore had us in its grip," Worsley wrote.

BELOW: One misstep, and a man could vanish into a crevasse.

One day, while they were cutting southward through the middle of the glacier, Adams said, impatiently, "I fundamentally disagree with the route we are taking." He pointed to a distant part of the glacier, saying, "We should be over there." Gow argued that they should maintain their course. Worsley feared dissension as much as a misguided route, and he said sternly to Adams, "Look, mate, we need to keep heading southward and upward."

Adams quietly relented. "Henry had a calm authority," Adams recalled. "He made crisp decisions. Sometimes they were right, sometimes they were wrong. You just didn't know, because you were walking through a maze. But he would make those decisions, having listened and consulted with us, so it made it very easy to follow him."

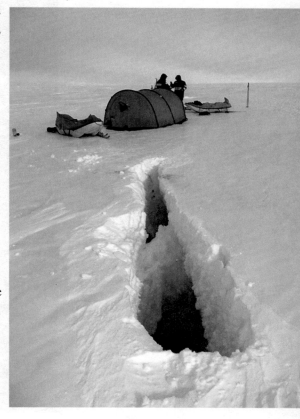

Traversing the Beardmore Glacier.

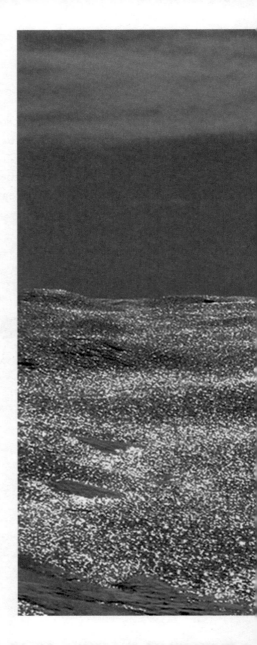

On December 24, after nine days of climbing, they reached the top of the glacier. To the west, they could see the Adams Mountain Range, named for Henry Adams's great-grandfather. In a broadcast, Worsley said, "It's Christmas Eve, and today . . . we bade farewell to the Beardmore Glacier." He went on, "We certainly worked hard to gain each mile, and that's why I find it such a rewarding phase of the journey."

On Christmas morning, instead of their usual breakfast of freeze-dried porridge, the team prepared a special meal of sausages, bacon, and beans. Later, they emulated the holiday celebration that Shackleton and his men had shared, lighting cigars and swallowing a teaspoon each of crème de menthe. Worsley called home and spoke to Joanna and Alicia, wishing them a merry Christmas. Alicia, who had painted on his skis U R THE BEST DAD EVER, asked him what it was like to experience a white Christmas, and said that she missed him dearly. Yet Max, who was still wrestling with his father's absence, refused to come to the phone.

Worsley then called his own father, hoping to share the news that he had reached the top of the glacier. But Richard Worsley, who was now eighty-five years old, had dementia, and when his son reminded him that he was in Antarctica he said, "What are you doing *there*?"

THE FOLLOWING MORNING, THE FORTY-THIRD DAY OF THE expedition, Worsley, Adams, and Gow began the next stage of their journey. They had travelled four hundred and eighty-nine nautical miles, and if they were to reach Shackleton's farthest point on January 9, two weeks away, they needed to cover as much as sixteen nautical miles each day. In a broadcast on December 27, Worsley echoed the words of Shackleton: "Please God, ahead of us is a clear road to the Pole."

But, as they ascended the Titan Dome, they confronted the most brutal conditions yet: hurricane-force gales, and a wind-chill temperature of minus sixty degrees. The cold air singed the men's lungs as if they were breathing fire. During a broadcast on December 28, Gow reported, "We were welcomed with our worst whiteout yet," adding, "All we could see were the tips of our skis."

Worsley kept a vigilant eye on his companions. They were almost unrecognizable from the young professionals who had set out from London. Their skin clung to their skulls and their eyes were sunken; they had wild beards and untamed hair that gleamed with ice. Because of the whiteouts, Adams was suffering from motion sickness. "I was moving and the surface was moving," he recalled. "It was like being trapped inside a Ping-Pong ball on a boisterous ocean." Gow, who had developed frostbite on his face, blasted blues songs into his earbuds—struggling, as he put it, to maintain a "sense of sanity."

BELOW: Burrowed into the tent,
amid freezing, gale-force winds.

Worsley tried to stay upbeat and comfort the others, lending a hand with their equipment or giving them Shackleton's compass to carry for good luck. But by December 31 it was Worsley who was suffering and struggling to keep pace. His body could not maintain sufficient body fat. "My days were fast turning into a raw, bare-knuckle fight against fatigue," he wrote. "Energy just poured from

my body, to be snatched away and dissipated by the wind. My legs would not work any faster. Each stride of the ski seemed locked at a precise distance. I could go no faster, just slower and slower."

On New Year's Day, he was again lagging. Adams waited for him to catch up and said, "General, let me carry some of your load."

Despite the pact they had made at the start of the journey, Worsley said, "I won't have it. We are all completely done in, so why should you?" He insisted, "I'll find a way. It's my problem to sort out." Pointing to his temple with his gloved hand, he added, "The answer lies here."

He was, he knew, blinded by pride; as he later wrote, he could not be seen as "admitting to weakness." And, rather than accept Adams's assistance, he discarded his emergency supply of food, which lightened his load by a few ounces. He recognized that it was a risky move: "I would go hungry . . . if we arrived at the Pole after 18 January."

Inside the tent on January 5, he opened the envelope that Joanna had given him. Some of the notes contained inspiring quotations, and he read aloud one from Winston Churchill: "We are masters of our fate, that the task which has been set before us is not above our strength; that its pangs and toils are not beyond our endurance. As long as we have faith in our cause and an unconquerable will to win, victory will not be denied us."

"Read it again, General," Adams asked.

"My days were fast turning into a raw, bare-knuckle
fight against fatigue," Worsley noted.

Worsley did, and then they all passed out.

The next day, during another whiteout, Adams got such severe
motion sickness that he began vomiting. Though Worsley had
never felt, in his own words, "so empty, so feeble and so beaten,"
he told Adams that he would switch sleds with him, given that
Adams's sled, which was carrying unused fuel canisters, was
heavier. Worsley then forged ahead at his fastest pace in days.
"Henry relied on force of mind," Adams recalled. There was
still a chance for them to make the ninety-seven-mile mark on

schedule. But on January 7, with just two days to go, another storm descended, and they were enveloped in the white darkness. Worsley explained to the others that they could either keep going or sit out the storm. But if they waited they would miss the anniversary. "I want to go on," Worsley said. But he stressed that the decision had to be unanimous.

"No question," Gow said.

"C'mo-o-on!" Adams cried.

During the next two days, the storm abated, and they covered more than twenty-five nautical miles. On January 9, they barrelled ahead for six hours. Then Worsley took out his GPS and gripped it, as he put it, "like an old man carefully carrying a cup of tea." As Gow and Adams anxiously looked on, Worsley shuffled around until the GPS connected with satellites and coordinates flashed on the screen: 88°23'S, 162°E.

"That's it!" he yelled, slamming his poles into the ground. "We've made it!" The men looked around, examining the place that had long consumed their imaginations, and which had lured them nearly to their demise. All they could see was barren ice—their grail was no more than a geographical data point. As Adams later put it, "What is Antarctica other than a blank canvas on which you seek to impose yourself?"

The temperature was minus thirty-one degrees, too cold to linger. But Worsley planted a British flag and arranged a group photograph similar to one that Shackleton had taken with his

Shackleton's team took a picture at 88°23'S—the southernmost point anyone had yet reached. Worsley's crew re-created the photo a hundred years later.

party. Adams was on the left, as his great-grandfather had been; Gow was in the middle; and Worsley stood on the right, in Shackleton's place.

Worsley kept thinking about the predicament that Shackleton had faced a hundred years earlier. Shortly before reaching the ninety-seven-mile mark, Shackleton had written in his diary, "I cannot think of failure yet. I must look at the matter sensibly and consider the lives of those who are with me. I feel that if we go on too far it will be impossible to get back over this surface, and then all the results will be lost to the world." He added, "Man can only do his best, and we have arrayed against us the strongest forces of nature." When he finally made the decision to retreat, on January 9, he wrote, "We have shot our bolt."

Worsley said to Gow and Adams, "I simply cannot contemplate them just turning round and heading back the way they had just come."

As Worsley and his companions continued toward the Pole, they were no longer following in Shackleton's steps. To their relief, they began descending in altitude, their sleds, lightened from the consumption of food, scooting easily behind them. After eight days, they had covered ninety-two nautical miles, a reminder of just how close Shackleton had been to realizing his dream. That night, Worsley went for his stroll, wobbling on bone-thin legs. He was not a religious man, but the landscape stirred him. As Adams put it, "Henry felt the spirituality of the Antarctic."

The next morning, the men broke camp, and embarked on the remaining five nautical miles. In the distance, they could finally see a signpost: the smudged outline of the Amundsen-Scott South Pole Station, a U.S. scientific-research base. After a few hours, Worsley noticed that his skis were moving in tracks that had been etched by snowmobiles. Then he saw, dumped in a pile on the ice, a broken washing machine, a mattress, and crushed boxes. The scentless air became infused with the sharp odors of fried food and petroleum; occasionally, a military plane roared overhead. "We had been thrust back into the world we had left behind," Worsley wrote.

In front of the research station, protruding from the ice, was a gleaming metal rod, about waist-high, topped with a brass globe.

Scientists at the base used it as a marker of the South Pole—the place where all the lines of longitude converge, and where the Earth doesn't rotate. Because the rod was planted on a shifting ice sheet, it had to be moved several feet each year, to return to the Pole's precise location.

On January 18, at 4:32 P.M., after sixty-six days, Worsley and his companions—emaciated, with icicles dripping from their beards—reached out and grasped the rod. As the journey had approached its end, Worsley had felt tears freezing under his eyes: he had not experienced such joy and relief since he was a little boy. But now Worsley, whom Adams called an "absolute bang-on natural leader," laughed and hollered and embraced the others. Only a few years earlier, they had been strangers, yet they had learned to trust one another with their lives. What's more, Worsley believed, they had mastered the seemingly impossible by adhering to the lessons of Shackleton; they had conquered through endurance. In a broadcast, Worsley announced, "I'm calling you from ninety degrees south, the South Pole!" Then he took out Shackleton's compass, lifted the lid, and let the needle spin to a stop.

Adams, Worsley, and Gow at the South Pole.

VII | THE INFINITE BEYOND

W ORSLEY DIDN'T THINK THAT HE WOULD EVER GO back to Antarctica again. He happily returned to the Army and relished being with his family. But he gradually began to feel again the "lure of little voices." In his commonplace book, he wrote down a quote, from the Norwegian polar explorer Fridtjof Nansen, that seemed to address his own compulsion to subject himself to more suffering: "Why? On account of the great geographical discoveries, the important scientific results? Oh no; that will come later, for the few specialists. This is something all can understand. A victory of human mind and human strength over the dominion and powers of Nature; a deed that lifts us above the great monotony of daily life; a view over shining plains, with lofty mountains against the cold blue sky, and lands covered by ice-sheets of inconceivable extent . . . the triumph of the living over the stiffened realm of death."

In 2012, Worsley launched a new expedition, to mark the centennial of the race between Amundsen and Scott to the South Pole. Gow and Adams, who had married and settled down with families, declined to go, and so Worsley drew recruits from the military. He and a partner, Lou Rudd, followed the trail of Amundsen and raced against another party, which took the route of Scott. Once more, Worsley proved an extraordinary commander—Rudd called him a "true inspiration"—and they won the nine-hundred-mile contest, which raised nearly three hundred thousand dollars for a Royal British Legion fund that assists wounded soldiers.

Worsley had become the first person to trace the two classic routes to the South Pole. *Outside* hailed him as "one of the great polar explorers of our time," and a reporter described him as a "pioneer of the possible." Worsley, who had recently published *In Shackleton's Footsteps,* gave lectures on exploration and leadership, becoming that rare apostle whose life seems to affirm his master's teachings.

In 2013, he was stationed in Washington, D.C., as the British liaison to U.S. Special Operations Forces. It was his final

111

A message Worsley carved into
the ice on his second expedition.

military posting: in October of 2015, after more than three and a half decades of service, he would be fifty-five, at that time the mandatory retirement age. Joanna had accompanied him to the States, and she sensed his mind drifting. "Are you doing another expedition?" she asked.

He said that the centenary of Shackleton's *Endurance* expedition would coincide with his retirement, and that he was considering an attempt of the trans-Antarctica crossing that Shackleton had planned before the sinking of his ship. What's more, Worsley hoped to make the nine-hundred-nautical-mile journey by himself, and without assistance, something that had never been done. Paul Rose, a former base commander for the British Antarctic Survey, which conducts scientific research in the region, called such a trek "unheard of," and another explorer deemed it an "almost inhuman challenge." For Worsley, the expedition represented the culmination of all his energies. Not only would it be his longest, hardest, and most punishing quest; he would have to survive entirely on his own wits.

Henry, though, told Joanna that he would return to Antarctica only if she approved. He was sensitive to the toll that his expeditions had taken on their family. He often struggled to express his emotions—the tumult that he had kept masked, even as it drove him—and in his book he had included a passage that seemed intended for his family, a way to convey what he could not say directly. "Looking back now, I realize that I lost track of where my real priorities should lie," he wrote. "I can see now that I was not dividing up the time sensibly and making my family feel important and special." He went on, "Passion for something can so easily tip into obsession, which is a dangerous thing, especially when those affected are the very people who so loyally 'stand and wait.'"

Joanna, who often joked that the Antarctic was her husband's "mistress," had expected that, upon his retirement, they would no longer be apart. But she had never tried to limit his aspirations— "He went with my blessings everywhere," she once told a reporter—and she understood how much the proposed trip meant to him. And Henry wasn't just doing it for himself—he hoped to raise a hundred thousand dollars for the Endeavour Fund, the other charity for injured soldiers. As he later put it, "I want to leave a financial legacy to assist my wounded mates." And so she gave Worsley her backing. The children were equally supportive. Max, who would be twenty-one by the time of the expedition, and who was helping to build ships in the South of France, had come to terms with his father's adventurist spirit, and even lionized him for it. They talked about eventually doing a polar journey together. "Everyone dreams, but Dad's the guy who goes out and achieves them," Max said.

In the fall of 2015, before Henry departed on the expedition, he and Joanna travelled to Greece. While visiting ancient sites and drinking wine at tavernas, they plotted out the things they

Max Worsley supported his father's later
expeditions, and even trained with him.

would do when he returned.
They would go to India and
teach underprivileged children,
and travel to Venice, where he
could study art and she could
do charity work. Max recalled,
"Mom was waiting twenty-five
years for the moment when he
left the Army and they could
do these things together."

Worsley no longer journeyed
in obscurity, and his plan
received admiring news
coverage. INTREPID EX-ARMY OFFICER IS SET FOR ANTARCTIC
TREK, the Glasgow *Herald* announced. A *Washington Post* headline
declared that Worsley would be ALL ALONE ON THE COLDEST
CONTINENT. Worsley was interviewed by *National Geographic* and
by the BBC, whose announcer said, "You must be mad to do it."
Prince William invited Worsley to Kensington Palace and signed
a Union Jack for him to carry with him on his trip, which was
similar to the one that King George V had given to Shackleton
before he departed.

On October 20, Joanna drove him to Heathrow Airport. She
was more worried about this expedition than any other, given
his age and the lack of help. In a video that Worsley posted on

Alicia, Henry, Joanna, and Max Worsley at Kensington
Palace, holding the flag signed by Prince William.

his website, he had spoken of
the risks of journeying solo.
The biggest threat, he said, was
falling into a crevasse: no one
could pull him out or call for
rescue. The other major threats,
he said, were a "severe medical
injury" and "severe weather." But
he believed that his meticulous
preparations would mitigate the
risks. While travelling alone, he
noted, "there is no one there to
compare thoughts with and seek
their opinions on, but I want to do this on my own." He later put
the matter even more starkly: "Success or failure of this journey is
completely up to me."

At the terminal, Joanna broke down, and he repeated what he
always told her: "Better a live donkey than a dead lion." Then he
kissed her and said, "Onwards!"

THIS TIME, WORSLEY'S ROUTE WAS TO BEGIN ON BERKNER
Island, an icebound chunk of rock off the Atlantic coast of
Antarctica, south of Chile. From there, he would trek five hundred
and seventy nautical miles to the South Pole. Then, heading in

the reverse direction from the one he had followed with Gow and Adams, he would ascend the Titan Dome and make his way down to the rim of the Ross Ice Shelf, on the Pacific side. This second section would cover three hundred and thirty nautical miles, and he estimated that the expedition would take him nearly eighty days. He was determined to finish before February, when winter set in and the conditions became too perilous for a rescue plane to land; even ALE shut down in winter. At that point, there would be no exit.

Worsley had hoped to fly to Antarctica shortly after arriving in Punta Arenas, on October 21. But foul weather—"our lord and master at the moment," as he called it—forced ALE to delay his flight for a week, and then another. "Greetings from Patience Camp," he reported on his broadcast. "Unfortunately, this is Patience Camp in Chile."

By the time he reached Berkner Island, on November 13, he was significantly behind schedule. He would need to arrive at the South Pole by January 1, 2016—a gruelling pace. Within moments of exiting the plane, he was packing his sled, which, because of the length of the journey, weighed three hundred and twenty-five pounds—even more than on his expedition with Gow and Adams. "Really worried about weight," he had written earlier, in his diary. Noting that "anxiety builds," he reminded himself that he needed to "banish negative thoughts."

He pushed off, and heard a familiar symphony: the poles

crunching on the ice, the sled creaking over ridges, the skis swishing back and forth. When he paused, he was greeted by that silence which seemed unlike any other. His doubts soon dissipated, and after a brief baptismal trek he made camp. The sun was shining and the temperature was a balmy nineteen degrees. "So, so happy to be back," he wrote in his diary. "Many days of struggle ahead but a glorious start. My spirits lifted as soon as I got going. I thought, 'I can do this.'" In his broadcast, he described Antarctica as the "best place on Earth right now."

The next morning, he began what he called his "first full day in the saddle." He trekked for eight hours, listening to tracks by David Bowie, Johnny Cash, and Meat Loaf and pondering what he might say, upon his return, in a lecture about the trip. He covered a good ten nautical miles, but it was a shock to his system. "First few days really are hell—never forget that," he wrote. If he focused on the length of his journey, he would never make it, and so he concentrated on immediate tasks. "It's just chipping away at it, bit by bit, and dealing with the moment," he later said on a broadcast. On the third day, after crossing the eighty-first degree of latitude, he convened a one-man meeting of the Malt Whiskey Appreciation Society, downing a shot of liquor, which he had cooled with snow. He knew that more and more people were following his broadcasts, including schoolchildren—"young explorers," he called them—and, despite his exhaustion, he took time each evening to relay updates and respond to inquiries that

The Weddell Sea, home to Berkner Island,
where Worsley began his solitary journey.

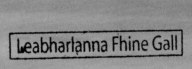

had been sent to him. He answered questions about whether he had seen any animal life ("sadly not"), about his favorite freeze-dried meal (spaghetti Bolognese), about his least favorite time of day (preparing to set off in the morning) and his favorite (climbing into his tent after a long march). He was asked which actor should portray him in a movie about his adventures. Admitting that his answer offered a "strong exposé of my vanity," he suggested Matt Damon for his younger self and Anthony Hopkins for his older self. He even replied to a question about how he went to the loo. "If you need to pee, throw your back to the wind, unzip, and have a pee," he explained. "Really not a big deal about that. On the other hand, if you need to go No. 2, you need to be a little more organized, particularly if there's a strong wind, which, generally, there is. This time, you face into the wind. You make sure that you've grabbed your outer trousers, your long johns, your pants, and you drop them as quickly as possible." One evening, after answering several queries, he playfully signed off from "somewhere" in "a complete whiteout."

By the end of the first week, he had travelled nearly seventy nautical miles. His body, he reported to listeners, was in remarkably good shape. He'd just enjoyed a hot meal of chicken cacciatore, with rice pudding for dessert. "I am now off to my sleeping bag," he said.

THEN, AS ON SHACKLETON'S *ENDURANCE* EXPEDITION, everything began to go wrong. On November 22, a little more than a week into his journey, he was engulfed in a whiteout and was pinned down in his tent. "Proper Antarctic storm!" he wrote in his diary, noting that there was no chance of moving forward that day. The next morning, the gusts felt strong enough to hurl a small dog; one of the tent poles broke, and he had to repair it. "A salutary reminder just who is in control around here," he said of the conditions. "Trespassers will be punished."

He emerged on November 24, and found himself plowing through a dust bowl of ice in which all he could see, hour after hour, was his compass strapped to his chest and his skis with their metronomic rhythm—an experience that he described as "miserable, mind-numbing, monochromatic monotony." He was ascending a section of the Transantarctic Mountains, and on November 25 he came upon a steep slope of ice that rose hundreds of feet. He tried to climb with his crampons, but the sled wouldn't move. Again, he tried. Again, it wouldn't budge.

If he didn't keep moving, he would freeze. He decided to lighten his sled, and unloaded most of his bags of food and stored them on a flat part of the ice. Then he began to climb. When he reached the top of the ridge, gasping for air behind his face mask, he deposited what he'd dragged up. After a short rest, he scaled back down to retrieve the rest. He made trip after trip.

Once, in the poor visibility, he failed to notice the scar of a

BELOW: "Trespassers will be punished," Worsley said.

crevasse and his foot broke through the surface. He felt himself slipping into the hole, which was widening around him. He grabbed the edge and clung to it, dangling over an abyss, before he hauled himself up. When he peered into the chasm, he wrote in his diary, he "suddenly felt very alone, vulnerable and scared."

His body was weakening more rapidly than on his previous expeditions. Not only was the sled heavier; he constantly had to break track, and he had to carry out alone the tiresome tasks of making camp each night and packing up in the morning.

On November 30, after trekking for nearly three weeks and traversing a hundred and sixty-five nautical miles, he reported that

he had "aching shoulders, lower-back pain, very snotty nose . . . and coughing due to breathing in cold air." He developed a rash on his groin. His feet were covered in bruises and blisters, and he took a knife to his boots, hoping to smooth the lining and alleviate the pain. One day, he suffered from a mysterious stomach ache, which was aggravated by the sled harness yanking at his waist.

Though he usually maintained a buoyant tone in his broadcast, he was more despairing in his diary. "It was a real physical battle with fatigue," he wrote, adding, "I was stopping literally every minute or so to catch my breath or just get ready for the next exertion required." Two nights later, after another whiteout, he lamented that he hadn't had enough strength "to pull the sledge through" the storm. His diary entries became a litany of suffering: "hard day"; "a very difficult day"; "a brutal day"; "awful day—floundering around in a complete whiteout"; "another awful day—worse than yesterday"; "swimming against a strong tide"; "still swimming against the tide"; "totally spent and demoralized." Each morning, he unzipped the flap of his tent and peeked out, hoping for clear skies, only to behold what he called "more of the white darkness." At times, he could not even discern the tips of his skis through the murk, which, he wrote, was as "thick as clotted cream."

On December 1, he marched into what he described as "the mother of all storms." Trudging uphill, with his head bowed against a fusillade of ice pellets, he moved at less than a mile per hour. After many hours, he abruptly paused. "I sat huddled on my sledge, down jacket on, wondering whether to go or to stop," he later recalled. It was so windy that he did not know if he could set up his tent, and so he resumed trekking. "My hands took a battering, and often I had to stop to give them some warmth," he said. "And the light was so flat that on two occasions, immediately after stopping, I fell straight over, such is the disorienting effect it has on your senses."

The next day, he blindly skied over a ridge, and the sled overtook him and pulled him down. His head and back and legs slammed against the ice. The sled flipped over twice, dragging him for twenty yards. He lay splattered on the ice, cursing. When he got to his feet, he nervously checked his fuel canisters. One crack and he would be doomed, but there were none, and, conscious of time slipping away, he untangled his harness and set off again.

AND INCREDIBLY, DESPITE EVERY OBSTACLE AND EVERY calamity, he was on track to reach the South Pole around New Year's Day. Nothing seemed to stop him. One morning, he forged on even when the conditions were so awful that he conceded that it was "crazy" to set off. Another time, he wrote in his diary, "I just can't go further—I don't have it in me." And yet he rose the next day and marched onward. On December 18, the thirty-sixth day, he walked more than seventeen nautical miles, a remarkable trek that took him fifteen hours. After another punishing day—which he described as a "combination of eating, bending, driving, tying, pushing, bracing, draining, swearing, pausing and despairing"—he told himself, "I just have to accept it and keep moving."

His existence had been reduced to a single purpose: making his mileage. When approaching sastrugi, he commanded himself to "attack, attack, attack." After one such battle, he wrote proudly in his diary that he had stormed "the ramparts of every piece that

Each day, Worsley beheld "more of the white darkness."

Worsley celebrated after passing
another degree of latitude.

was unfortunate enough to get in my way." He added, "The sledge, now a battering ram and not a burden, smashed through all in its path." When he was asked by his radio listeners how he persevered, he said that it was less about physical prowess than about how "strong your mind and will are—hours at the gym cannot prepare you."

Robert Swan, a British adventurer who had trekked to both poles, was monitoring Worsley's journey, and expressed awe at his daily progress. In an audio message posted on Worsley's website, on December 5, Swan said, "His average is fantastic," adding, "He's facing some quite odd conditions, but, being Henry, he's slugging it out." In a second message, posted later that month, Swan described Worsley proceeding as if a traffic light were glowing in front of him: "Very, very rarely in your mind do you ever see the color green, for the simple reason if you're in green you're probably not pushing hard enough. . . . You're thinking about your feet, your legs, your calves, your hips, your arms, your neck, your shoulders, and you're constantly doing these checks to see whether everything's OK. . . . As Henry has said, as he moves towards those last few hours every day, you can feel that he's pushing into the red zone. And the red zone is not a place to stay in, because in the red zone your body is starting to eat itself. You're much more likely to get frostbite. So you live on the edge of the orange, occasionally push into the red, and then, very sensibly, he comes back off the red, back into the orange. And hopefully, when he's into his sleeping bag and speaking to us, you know he's back into the green."

By Christmas Day, Worsley was nearly within a hundred nautical miles of the Pole. Prince William broadcast a message, saying, "We're thinking of you at the Christmas period as you're lugging all your kit up and down the slopes and the hills of the southern Atlantic in the Antarctic." Worsley opened a package that Joanna and the children had given him. Inside were miniature versions of traditional Christmas sweets: a mincemeat pie and a fruitcake. Alicia had written him a note that quoted lyrics from *The Jungle Book:* "Look for the bare necessities / The simple bare necessities / Forget about your worries and your strife." And Joanna had included a sample of Amouage Journey Man cologne. "I figured his tent would be so smelly by then," she recalled.

On his broadcast, Worsley said, "Packages from home, especially at times like this, no matter where you are in the world, carry special meaning. And none more so for me this morning."

Using his satellite phone, he called Joanna and Alicia, in London, and then Max, in France. Throughout the journey, Worsley had made a record in his diary of virtually every communication that he had had with them. Once, after speaking to Joanna, he wrote, "I do love her so much." Another time, after he received a text from Alicia saying "I am thinking of you constantly, and love you more than ever," he jotted down, "Sweet text from Shrimp"—his nickname for her. And he noted that a conversation one morning with Max had "lifted my spirits." On Christmas Day, he wrote in his diary, "Lovely to hear their voices."

Despite the holiday, Worsley marched twelve nautical miles. As he lay in his tent that night, he lit a cigar, the sweet smoke filling the air, and ate his Christmas treats. It was, he said, like a "little heaven."

Soon, he was almost at nine thousand feet, the elevation of the South Pole. He was so tired that once, while sitting on his sled during a snack break, he nodded off, even though the wind-chill temperature was minus twenty-two. "I may be drained of all power and energy," he reported on a broadcast. "But I still seem to have the will that says, to my heart and nerves and sinews, *Hold on*." He kept telling himself, "Keep your eyes on the prize."

On January 2, only a day behind schedule, he reached the Pole. He was greeted by a group of well-wishers from the scientific-research station. They were the first people he had seen in fifty-one days. But this was not the climax of his journey—it was only the end of the first phase—and, because he was making his trek unaided, he couldn't go inside the base to receive a hot meal or even to take a bath. "It was weird arriving here and not stopping," he wrote in his diary, adding, "Very tempting to stay at Pole—eat and sleep." But he set up his camp as usual, maintaining his self-imposed exile.

During his broadcast, he told his listeners, "I owe so much to all of you for your support in getting me this far. I cannot emphasize too strongly just how much it has urged me on over the darker days, of which there have been many. But those I have to thank most are Joanna, Max, and Alicia." His voice cracked. "They have been with me every step of the way, each with a warm hand in the small of my back, lifting me when I am down, strengthening me when I am weak, and filling me when I'm empty. I owe them everything." He concluded, "At the southerly point where the world spins on—good night."

IN LONDON, JOANNA LISTENED TO HIS BROADCASTS EACH evening before falling asleep. Shortly before Christmas, she was interviewed by a reporter from the *Daily Express*, and she said, "Henry was away abroad a lot in his army days so we've been used to separations . . . but I miss him much more now. I do worry about him because I know how frail he is getting—he does lose a huge amount of weight and he has had a really rough time with the weather." She went on, "He is so determined. In my head I know there's no way he won't succeed, even if he has to walk all day and night. He has enormous mental strength." She was overcome: "He's an amazing man—isn't it wonderful to be married to someone like that?"

Worsley estimated that it would take him about three weeks to complete the rest of his journey, and he hoped that the hardest part was behind him. In his diary, he had written, "Just pray going North is that much easier." Yet, as he climbed the Titan Dome, he found the ascent to be "a killer." He had lost more than forty pounds, and his unwashed clothing hung on him heavily. "Still very weak—legs are stick thin and arms puny," he noted in his diary. His eyes had sunk into shaded hollows. His fingers were becoming numb. His Achilles tendons were swollen. His hips were battered and scraped from the constantly jerking harness. He had broken his front tooth biting into a frozen protein bar, and told ALE that he looked like a pirate. He was dizzy from the altitude, and he had bleeding hemorrhoids.

On January 7, he woke in the middle of the night with another stomachache. "I felt pretty awful," he admitted on his broadcast. "The weakest I felt in the entire expedition." The earbuds on his iPod had broken, leaving him in silence. "I feel alone," he confessed on a broadcast, adding, "Occasionally, it would be nice to have somebody to talk to about the day."

He kept thinking that he would soon reach the top of the Titan Dome. "I'll be okay if the promised 'downhill' materializes," he wrote in his diary. But the peak eluded him—he was trapped in an infinite beyond. On January 11, he told his listeners, "I'm desperate to go down and into air thick enough to breathe."

Listening to the broadcasts, Joanna was increasingly concerned. "I felt in his voice this exhaustion and sadness," she recalled. He had no companion to tell him that he had remained too long in the red zone; nor was he held back by the worry that his actions might jeopardize the lives of others. And he was confident that he could do what he always had done: prevail through unbending will. In his commonplace book, he had once written down a quote, from the cyclist Lance Armstrong, that said, "Losing and dying: it's the same thing."

132

"I feel alone," Worsley admitted on a broadcast.

And so Worsley pressed on, muttering to himself a line from Tennyson's poem "Ulysses": "To strive, to seek, to find, and not to yield." Once, he looked up in the sky and saw, through his frozen goggles, a dazzling sun halo. On the edge of the circle, there were intense bursts of light, as if the sun were being splintered into three fiery balls. He knew that the phenomenon was caused by sunlight being refracted through a scrim of ice particles. Yet, as he stumbled onward through the void, he wondered if the light was actually some guiding spirit, like the "fourth man" that Shackleton had spoken of. Perhaps Worsley, too, had pierced the "veneer of outside things"—or perhaps his mind was simply unravelling. His diary entries had become sparer and darker: "So breathless . . . I am fading . . . hands/fingers are forever shutting down . . . wonder how long they will last."

On January 17, he staggered through a whiteout, pulling his sled for sixteen hours. When he stopped, it was late evening, and he struggled to build his camp again—to plant the tent poles in the ice, to unload his food, to light the cooker, to melt snow for water. "It's now one o'clock in the morning," he said in his broadcast. "In sum, it's been a punishing day." He continued, "What little energy I have left . . ." His voice faded in and out.

Joanna panicked upon hearing the broadcast. She called many of Worsley's close friends, asking if someone should ask ALE to dispatch a rescue plane. They thought that Worsley would be OK, given his experience and abilities, and that he should be the one to make such a call. Robert Swan, in one of his earlier broadcasts, had noted that Worsley had on his belt "a wonderful, unbelievable" Iridium satellite telephone, adding, "If he does have a problem, he can hit the button and get some support and rescue very, very quickly."

On January 19, after man-hauling through another storm, Worsley was too tired to give a broadcast, and with his frozen hand he scribbled only a few words in his diary, the writing almost illegible: "Very desperate . . . slipping away . . . stomach . . . took painkillers." He was incontinent, and repeatedly had to venture outside to squat in the freezing cold. His body seemed to be eating itself.

The next day, the sixty-ninth day of his journey, he could drag his sled for only a few hours. He built his tent and collapsed inside. At one point, he called Max on the satellite phone, waking him in the middle of the night in France. All Henry kept saying was "I just want to hear your voice, I just want to hear your voice."

Max told him, "You will always be a polar warrior in my eyes. You just need to pull out and come home."

On the morning of January 21, Joanna spoke to him. He was suffering from, as she put it, "complete shutdown." He couldn't even muster the energy to boil water or to brush his teeth, and she pleaded with him to call ALE and evacuate. "You've absolutely got to call them," she said.

He told her that, though he wasn't going to leave the tent, he needed some time to think through what to do next. He spent the day wrestling with his predicament, wondering what Shacks would do. Worsley had written in his diary, "Just want it all to end," adding, "Miss everybody badly." But the GPS had informed him that he had finally passed the apex of the Titan Dome, and had started to descend. History was within his grasp. In his diary, he had written, "Never, ever give in." It echoed a lesson from one of the Shackleton self-help books, which Worsley had once posted on his website: "Never give up—there's always another move."

But maybe that was wrong. Hadn't Shackleton survived *because* he had realized that, at a certain point, he had no more moves and turned back? Unlike Scott and others who went to a polar grave, Shackleton reckoned with his own limitations and those of his men. He understood that not everything, least of all the Antarctic, can be conquered. And that within defeat there can still be triumph—the triumph of survival itself.

On January 22, after seventy-one days and a trek of nearly eight hundred nautical miles, Worsley pushed the button and called for the most expensive taxi ride in the world. "Greetings, everybody," he said on his broadcast. "When my hero Ernest Shackleton walked ninety-seven miles from the South Pole on the morning of January 9, 1909, he said he'd shot his bolt." Worsley continued, "Well, today I have to inform with some sadness that I, too, have shot my bolt. . . . My journey is at an end. I have run out of time and physical endurance—and a simple, sheer inability to slide one ski in front of the other. . . . My summit is just out of reach." But he sounded relieved: "I'll lick my wounds. I will heal over time, and I'll come to terms with the disappointment." His spirits were buoyed by the outpouring of donations to the Endeavour Fund, which had exceeded his goal and would eventually surpass a quarter of a million dollars. "It is incredible and does make me smile," he said. He explained that the rescue plane would arrive shortly, and that he was looking forward to a cup of hot tea. He concluded, "This is Henry Worsley, signing off, at journey's end."

He had already told Joanna of his decision, and she couldn't wait to see him and hold him. As she later noted, "Obviously, he will feel disappointed, but Shackleton never reached his goals, and what Henry has done is extraordinary." She notified Max and Alicia and many friends, all of whom expressed relief that he had decided to come home. Or, as Joanna thought of it: *He chose us.*

When the plane arrived, later on January 22, he rose proudly and walked under his own power, though he needed help climbing the stairs into the cabin. He knew that he had made the right decision: he had seen his naked soul. Worsley was flown to ALE's base camp, on the other side of Antarctica, where, according to a company report, he was "talking happily about home and his upcoming lecturing engagement." That evening, he called Joanna and said, "I'm having a cup of tea and I'm going to be fine."

BELOW: Flying to ALE's base camp.

"I love you so much," she said.

"Darling, I love you, too," he said, promising to call her the next morning.

AROUND TWO IN THE AFTERNOON ON JANUARY 23, THE phone rang. But it wasn't Henry—it was Steve Jones, ALE's expeditions manager. He explained that the doctors had discovered that Worsley was suffering from bacterial peritonitis, an infection of the thin tissue that lines the inner wall of the abdomen. It might have been caused by a perforated ulcer, and if an infection spread into his bloodstream it could produce septic shock. ALE had flown Worsley to a hospital in Punta Arenas, and he was being rushed into surgery. He was still talking about his family and his upcoming lecture, as if unable to comprehend the sudden turn of events. Hadn't he turned back? Jones asked Joanna if she wanted to speak

to him. She feared delaying the operation, and said no, promising to be on the next plane to Chile.

She caught the first flight out and arrived in Santiago, where she waited for a connecting flight to Punta Arenas. While she was in Santiago, she met the British ambassador to Chile, Fiona Clouder, who told Joanna that Henry's condition was grave. Joanna continued to get updates from the hospital, and was informed that his liver had failed. You can live without a liver, can't you? Joanna thought. Then she heard that his kidney had failed, and thought, Can't you live without a kidney? Then, just before Joanna was to board the plane for Punta Arenas, the ambassador got a call from the British Embassy. Afterward, Clouder knelt beside Joanna, held her hand, and said what Joanna already knew: Henry was dead.

Accompanied by the ambassador, Joanna flew to Punta Arenas. She went past city streets and pedestrians, but didn't see anything; it was as if she were in a whiteout. She was taken into a church: light filtering through stained-glass windows, a cross on the wall. In front of her was an open wooden casket. Henry was inside. She had been told that several rock specimens had been found in his possession when he was evacuated, which was so like him: to carry them even as he was struggling to pull his weight. She looked down at his face. "I was completely terrified," she recalled. "But he looked incredibly peaceful. Almost happy." She leaned over and kissed him, his skin still warm.

Joanna was filled with regrets. She wished that she had spoken to him before he had gone into surgery. She wished that he had abandoned his quest sooner, and that she had called ALE herself. "I'll feel guilty for the rest of my life," she said. She was facing "an absolute wall of pain," her own Antarctica.

Joanna called their children. Alicia, who had always shared some of her father's stoicism, nearly collapsed. Some time later, she looked through her father's writings about his journey and found a line that has stayed with her: "You are sitting on a large white plate looking out to the edge and I would draw myself back up into the sky and into space and look down and think of myself as this atom on an ice cube in the middle of nowhere." Long afterward, Max found himself waiting for his father to appear. "He was always the invincible man—not physically but mentally—and I still expect him to come back," he recalled. "I'm still waiting." Despite his grief, he was overwhelmed with pride when he thought of his father: "If I'm even half the man Dad turned out to be, I'd be so pleased." Whereas his father would ask himself, "What would Shacks do?," Max asked himself, "What would Dad do?"

When the news of Worsley's death reached Great Britain, Prince William said, "We have lost a friend, but he will remain a source of inspiration to us all." The press hailed Worsley as "one of the world's great polar explorers" and a "hero from a bygone age." He was posthumously awarded the Polar Medal, which had been given to Scott and Shackleton. In a Facebook post, Nancy F.

Koehn, the author of the book *Ernest Shackleton, Exploring Leadership*, wrote, "Worsley considered Shackleton his hero, and now we see Worsley as one of ours."

The funeral was held on February 11, 2016, at St. Paul's Church in Knightsbridge. Hundreds of people gathered, among them Prince William, General Nick Carter, Henry Adams, and Will Gow. In tribute to Worsley, many of the mourners wore brightly colored ties or scarves. Although Worsley's remains were cremated, there was a casket, draped with Polar Star white roses; his military medals had been placed on the lid, resting on an embroidered cushion that Worsley had sewn, depicting Shackleton and his men.

In a eulogy, Adams said of Worsley, "His exploits and the way in which he undertook them have quite rightly seen him portrayed as a hero. But I'm not sure he would have been entirely comfortable with that moniker. His heroism is just one part of the fabric of an incredibly rich character." He went on, "He was primarily a father and a husband. He was a soldier. He was an artist. A raconteur. I loved him as the kindest of friends and the most honorable of men. He had the most substance of any man I have ever met."

Max rose to speak. Tall and thin, with curly black hair and intense brown eyes, he was as striking a man as his father had been. Max recited the poem that he had written about Antarctica when he was thirteen years old and his father was embarking on his first expedition:

BELOW: Max, Joanna, and Alicia Worsley
visited South Georgia Island in 2017.

What beauty is seen through the mist of white snow,
The depths of Antarctica, where no one will go.
The biting wind will freeze thoughts from your mind,
And the deathless cold will leave you behind . . .

Now that it's morning the beauty shows,
And as the sun rises, Antarctica glows;
And as I leave this beautiful land,
The life beyond me starts to expand.

IN DECEMBER OF 2017, ALMOST TWO YEARS AFTER THE funeral, Joanna, Max, and Alicia travelled by boat to South Georgia Island. "I wanted to go to the place Henry so loved," Joanna said. They disembarked on the eastern shore of the island, where, beneath towering glaciers, there was a small wooden chapel built in 1913 by whalers from Norway.

Joanna and her children held a ceremony for Worsley in the chapel. After a while, they headed outside, and hiked up an icy slope. A light snow was falling, and Joanna had wrapped herself in the down coat that Worsley had worn on his final expedition. "I felt as if he was walking beside me," she recalled.

She and her children climbed until they reached a peak that overlooks the cemetery where Shackleton is buried. They had brought a wooden box, which Worsley had made for one of his expeditions. Inside were his ashes. At the chapel, Max, who had begun to contemplate attempting his own polar expedition, had recited the sonnet about Shackleton that his father had loved:

> All striving done and "life's set prize" attained:
> Not geographic goals, but greater far
> The pinnacles of leadership you gained.

Joanna and her children dug a hole and buried Worsley's ashes in the frozen earth.

ACKNOWLEDGMENTS

I could not have written this story without the support and generosity of the Worsley family. Joanna, Max, and Alicia are among the most extraordinary people I've ever encountered, and I feel so fortunate to have gotten to know them. Henry Worsley's mother, Sally, and his sister, Charlotte, were equally kind and patient, sharing with me their memories.

I'm also deeply grateful to many of Worsley's friends and colleagues who spoke to me. They include Henry Adams, Angie Butler, General Sir Nick Carter, Catherine Gale, Will Gow, and Bill Shipton. Many of the book's photographs were provided by Gale, Gow, and Shipton, and by Sebastian Copeland, Roger Pimenta, Lou Rudd, and the Worsley family. Hugh de Lautour allowed me to quote his poem about Shackleton. And David Rootes and Steve Jones of ALE never tired of helping me to understand the alien and astonishing nature of Antarctica.

I'm indebted to *The New Yorker*, where this story first appeared, and to my editors there, including the incomparable Daniel Zalewski, Dorothy Wickenden, Andrew Boynton, and, of course, David Remnick. David Kortava and Elizabeth Barber provided indispensable fact-checking.

Bill Thomas, my brilliant editor and publisher at Doubleday, had the vision to see how the narrative could be integrated with images that tell a story unto themselves. Because of him and all the miracle workers at the Knopf Doubleday Publishing Group, led by its chairman, Sonny Mehta, *The White Darkness* became the book you are now holding. I especially want to thank Todd Doughty, John Fontana, Suzanne Herz, Andy Hughes, Lorraine Hyland, Pei Koay, Maria Massey, and Margo Shickmanter.

As always, I'm grateful for the friendship and support of Kathy Robbins and David Halpern, at the Robbins Office, and of Matthew Snyder, at CAA.

Finally, I want to thank my wife, Kyra, and my children, Zachary and Ella. They have bolstered me in ways that I can never express in words.

IllUSTRATION CREDITS

ABOUT THE AUTHOR

David Grann is a staff writer at *The New Yorker* and the bestselling author of *The Lost City of Z* and National Book Award Finalist *Killers of the Flower Moon*, both of which were chosen as one of the best books of their respective year by *The New York Times*, *The Washington Post*, and other publications. He is also the author of *The Devil and Sherlock Holmes* and *The Old Man and the Gun*. His work has garnered several honors for outstanding journalism, including a George Polk Award and an Edgar Award.